Good running!

55½ *RUNNING*

TRAILS

OF THE SAN FRANCISCO BAY AREA

55½ RUNNING TRAILS

OF THE SAN FRANCISCO BAY AREA

BY TONY BURKE

HEYDAY BOOKS, BERKELEY

Acknowledgment
Many thanks to: Pete Castellanos for suggesting this project; Malcolm Margolin and the gang at Heyday Books for their skill, friendship and beer; Cec' Robertson and John Orear for lending me their camera equipment; countless runners for ideas and enthusiasm; and my non-running friends who displayed genuine interest in this endeavor.

Cover design: Sarah Levin
Photographs by the author.
Cartography, design, and production: Nancy McMichael

Printed in the United States of America.

10 9 8 7 6 5 4 3 2 1

Published by
Heyday Books
Box 9145
Berkeley, CA 94709

ISBN: 0-930588-22-3
Library of Congress Catalog Card: 85-080907

Dedication: *For my wife and friend, Nicole; an exceptionally patient and understanding woman.*

INTRODUCTION

Despite all the well-documented merits of running, even the hardiest of long-distance enthusiasts will occasionally admit to being bored. Not with the sport itself (perish the thought!), but with its setting. Most of us, from casual jogger to hundred-mile-per-week stalwart, fall victim to repetition: plodding the same two or three familiar routes near our home or workplace. Bound as we are during the week by work and family commitments, any significant variation in running location is difficult. So we grab our running shoes and take off for the umpteenth time around our personal circuit, grateful to be running at all. But weekends, vacations, and, perhaps, those gloriously long summer evenings, are for running free; discovering new, fresh runs, and enjoying the pure essence of the sport.

The Bay Area is rich in running opportunities, with many hundreds of miles of trails through parks, preserves, wildlife areas, and cities. The 56 trails selected for this publication are by no means the total of what the area has to offer. Instead, the book attempts to introduce places you may never have considered before—runs along the bay shore, over hills, through redwoods, around lakes, next to streams, on ocean beaches, or through unusual city streets. It tells you how to get to the run, what to expect when you arrive, and suggests and describes a specific route. In most cases the suggested route is only one of several alternatives, but it will serve you well as an introduction to an area. Distances, too, can usually be varied to suit your mood on any given day: lengthened to accommodate an improving fitness level; shortened due to the lingering effects of the previous night's party.

Characteristic Bay Area weather patterns can also work to our advantage. A runner can escape sweltering inland temperatures to run through a cooling fog at the Marin Headlands—or vice versa.

In addition to many out-of-the-ordinary runs, I have included a few old favorites: Lake Merced, Lafayette Reservoir, Lake Merritt, and the like. Already well-established with the runners living nearby, these runs have much to offer visitors from neighboring towns. Give them a whirl if you have the chance, and you'll soon learn that there is good reason for their popularity.

In the vast majority of these runs, automobile traffic ("the biped's bane") is noticeably absent. Instead, you are free to wander through shaded valleys and spacious meadows without fear of horn blowers and bottle throwers. Mother Nature, however, has a few irritants of her own; most notably poison oak. While every effort has been made to feature only well-maintained trails and fire roads. Caution is recommended, especially during hot summer months.

The information on trail conditions, water availability, restrooms, and other facilties reflects the way things were in the summer of '85. You may, however, find changes. If, on rare occasions, your path is closed for resurfacing, widening, or repair of erosion, you can usually find other routes nearby. Of more concern, especially on hot days, is water. It is advisable to have some with you on long runs, even when listed here as available. I would hate to suffer your wrath because park officials inexplicably disconnected the only water fountain for miles around.

Throughout this book I have emphasized trails which showcase the remarkable beauty of the Bay Area. The greater number of runs pass through rural land, forests, or along the shores of the bay. Yet even those winding through populated areas are not without charm, character, and beauty—no small praise in these days of hustle and highrise. One of my greatest pleasures in researching this book has been to find that in an area with a population in excess of 4,000,000, there are so many exciting, truly excellent trails to run. I invite you to try them all.

Tony Burke

CONTENTS

MARIN COUNTY

Mt. Tamalpais—Muir Woods

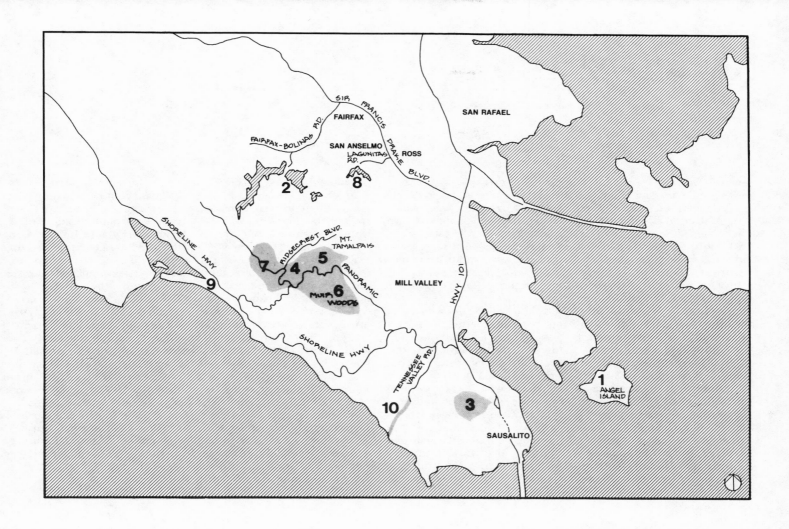

ANGEL ISLAND

Trail: *4.8 miles. Loop; gently rolling; paved and dirt; some shade. Views of bay area. Deer.*

General Description:

It's hard to imagine a finer location for a run than 740-acre Angel Island. Rising out of the bay to the 750-foot peak of Mt. Livermore, the island's steep hillsides are rich in natural history. Madrone, oak and bay trees are native to the area, while the eucalyptus, Douglas fir, and Monterey cypress have been introduced over the years. The wildlife is diverse, and prominently includes the notorious deer who insist on multiplying, despite the widely-publicized efforts to curtail them.

Runners come to Angel Island mainly for its pleasantly undulating five-mile perimenter trail. Circling this island on foot, you can enjoy fine running over an excellent surface while one view after another unfolds before you as if someone were opening the pages of a giant picture book.

Ferries from San Francisco and Tiburon are the only means of access to the island unless you own a boat yourself. All boats dock at Ayala Cove on the northwest side, near the park headquarters and the beach and picnic areas where most of the visitors spend their time.

Taking the clockwise direction on the perimeter trail from Ayala Cove, you soon become accustomed to the trail's roller-coaster traits. Mt. Tamalpais and the hillsides of Marin County can be seen to the west; it was from there that the coastal Miwok Indians would paddle their tule reed boats to this island for fishing and hunting. Rounding the point past Winslow Cove, you can see the Richmond-San Rafael Bridge across the bay. The buildings of the North Garrison will be off to your left; this area was used as an immigration processing station from 1910 until World War II, when it became a temporary detention camp for Japanese POWs.

Running downhill, looking toward the East Bay, you see the East Garrison, which served as a holding area for Spanish-American War veterans with contagious diseases and as a major embarkation point for American troops headed for the Pacific in World War II. Before this area was used as a military base, its cliffs were a source of fine sandstone for the new buildings of San Francisco.

An uphill stretch over a gravel surface is rewarded by a terrific look at the San Francisco skyline. Then it's downhill again, with the Golden Gate Bridge in the distance before you. Turning north on the final leg of the run, you will pass Camp Reynolds to your left, which played an important role as a depot for soldiers recruited to fight the Indian wars of the late 1800s. Once again Sausalito and Tiburon come into view and a final downhill will bring you to the end of the run.

The day is now yours. You can spend it exploring the empty batteries or the eerie buildings now inhabited only by the winds that often whip around the island. If the weather is good, you can picnic in one of the coves or climb to the top of Mt. Caroline Livermore (named for a Marin conservationist) and take full advantage of the lofty vantage point. During the summer, a snack bar can supply you with food and drink.

Directions to the Trail:

From downtown Tiburon, take the Angel Island Ferry to Ayala Cove.

From downtown San Francisco, take the Red & White Ferry from Pier 43½ to Ayala Cove.

Directions for the Run:

From the Ayala Cove ferry dock, take the path up past the visitor center to the perimeter trail. Run in a clockwise direction around the island and return to this spot.

Other Information:

Toilets and water at start/finish. Water on route.

Picnic areas; abandoned military installations; visitor center. At the visitor center, you can buy a park brochure for 50¢ which will explain some of the island's history and show a map of the perimeter trail. Some lightweight clothing to wear after the run is recommended.

Telephone numbers: Angel Island State Park, **(415)435-1915**; Angel Island Ferry from Tiburon, **(415)435-2131**; Red & White Fleet from Pier 43½ in San Francisco, **(415)546-2815**.

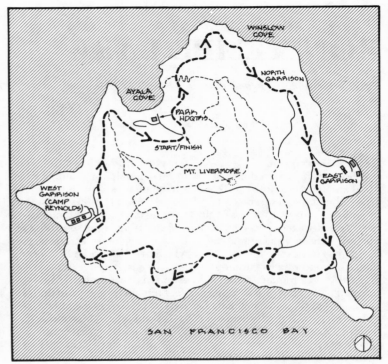

BON TEMPE LAKE

Trail: *4.1 miles. Loop; rolling; dirt; 40% shade. Views of lake and hillsides.*

General Description:

Below the northern slopes of Mt. Tamalpais lies Bon Tempe Lake, one of five reservoirs serving Marin County. Runners of all levels are attracted to its perimeter trail—those who know about it, that is. For despite the abundance of good-quality running trails, this area remains something of a secret except to local runners—and they're not telling.

I chose to include the Bon Tempe Lake Trail instead of its neighbors for several reasons: its medium distance, easy-to-follow route, nontaxing terrain, attractive scenery, and convenient amenities (good parking, portable toilets, and a water fountain about halfway into the run). Using this suggested route as a base, you can make exploratory trips to the other lakes and even to Mt. Tamalpais. Training runs can be increased to almost any distance over terrain which offers varying degrees of difficulty.

Beginning at the south end of the parking lot, you cross the dam which overlooks both Bon Tempe and the eastern edge of the larger Alpine Lake. On the far side you veer left and plunge into the coolness of pine trees, beginning the trek along the southern side of the lake. This is great running—trails soft underfoot amidst the cleansing fragrance of the forest, whose trees shield you from sun and wind. The trail bobs up, down and around, occasionally crossing narrow wooden bridges above creeks feeding the lake.

At the lake's eastern tip you pass over a bridge into a large picnic area. Next you pass a series of sluice gates, whose mechanisms look amazingly like anti-aircraft guns. On the northern edge of the lake, the scattered oaks offer little shade, but the water is clearly visible for much of the remaining distance. In several places the single file path drops to a few feet above the lake, and caution is required because of erosion to the bank. The lakeside route soon brings you to the parking lot and the end of this run.

Because the area is undeveloped, there is not too much to do after running except have a picnic. The towns of Fairfax and San Anselmo are near enough to provide refreshments. Or you can make a day of it and follow the Fairfax-Bolinas Road westward to the coast, Mt. Tamalpais, or Muir Woods. The drive alone is worthwhile, showcasing some of Marin's finest countryside.

Directions to the Trail:

From Sir Francis Drake Blvd. in Fairfax, take the Fairfax-Bolinas Road west and turn left on Sky Oaks Road. Continue past the ranger station. Where the road forks, go right to Bon Tempe Lake and park near the dam.

Directions for the Run:

From the parking lot, cross the dam and turn left on the far side (1). Follow the trail to the east end of the lake and cross the bridge. Keep to the left of Lagunitas Picnic Area (2). Staying near the water, cross the sluice gates onto the wider trail, ignoring trails to the right. Run beside the lake passing a trail off to the left (which deadends at the lake). Veer left at the next fork onto the narrow trail (3). From here on keep an eye out for exposed roots and other small obstacles. Continue beside the lake to the paved road (4), go left on it a short way, and at the white dots in the road turn left onto another narrow dirt path (5). Stay beside the water back to the dam and the parking lot.

Other Information:

Portable toilet at start/finish and at paved road on the east side of the lake. Toilets and water at Lagunitas Picnic Area. Possible parking fee.

Telephone number: Marin Municipal Water District, (415)924-4600.

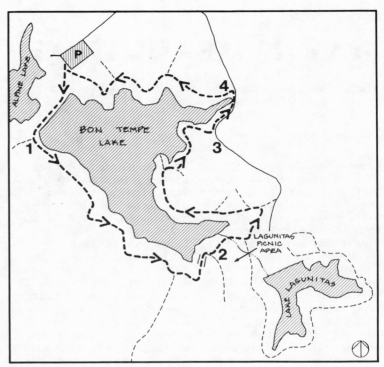

MARIN HEADLANDS

Trail: *5.5 miles. Loop; hills; dirt; exposed, wind and fog. Views of San Francisco and ocean. Birds and wildflowers.*

General Description:

North of the Golden Gate, rising from the Pacific Ocean, are the craggy bluffs and windswept hills of the Marin County Headlands. Over the years they've been home to cattle ranches and military installations. Now part of the Golden Gate National Recreation Area, the emphasis is on leisurely pursuits, such as hiking, bird watching, and, of course, running. Many well-surfaced trails wander the open hillsides and offer mile after mile of running opportunities for those who don't mind a climb or two. The absence of trees allows uncluttered views of the Pacific and, from higher elevations, of Mt. Tamalpais and Mt. St. Helena. The overall effect is a tremendous sense of freedom.

Setting off from the busy parking lot west of Hwy 101, you immediately wind uphill into a dense grove of eucalyptus on the steep quarter-mile Morning Sun Trail. Running on this trail is just about impossible, and you may want to walk, using the time to loosen up your muscles and to catch glimpses of the Sausalito Yacht Harbor, a picture of serenity far below. This trail ends at a wide dirt path, and you emerge into the open for the remainder of the run.

A series of ups and downs through chaparral on Bobcat Trail brings you to Miwok Trail. Miwok drops southward, revealing San Francisco's Golden Gate Park and perhaps ships far out to sea. The land, apparently barren at first, soon proves otherwise. Hawks sway overhead, black-tailed deer play hide-and-seek in the brush, and in the spring a chorus line of poppies dance around the trail and the entire valley comes alive with colorful wildflowers.

Miwok Trail descends to the valley floor, then almost immediately veers into Bobcat Trail. Beyond a row of eucalyptus, the trail begins to climb again, passing a wildflower garden of paintbrush, morning glories, and irises, which display a kaleidoscope of color when in bloom. Going gradually uphill, you return to Morning Sun Trail and the refreshing coolness of the forest. An effortless, gravity-propelled stroll down to the car is a pleasant change from the preceding climb.

A visit to the California Marine Mammal Center at Rodeo Lagoon provides an interesting post-run excursion. The stalwart group of people there, mostly volunteers, rescue injured marine mammals—seals, sea lions, dolphins, and even whales—stranded on the California coast. Many are brought here to Fort Cronkhite to be treated and hopefully released back into the ocean.

Solar energy is explained at the Golden Gate Energy Center near the beach, and numerous exhibits make this another rewarding stopoff. The adjacent GGNRA visitor center supplies information on the amazing variety of seminars, walks, and lectures offered to acquaint the public with the surroundings. Some of the activities are especially for children.

Directions to the Trail:

From Hwy 101 just south of Sausalito, take Spencer Ave./Monte Mar Dr. exit and park in one of the lots on either side of the freeway.

For an alternative starting point at Rodeo Lagoon, take Alexander Ave. exit, turn left onto Bunker Road, follow it through the tunnel to Fort Cronkhite Park Headquarters, and park.

Directions for the Run:

From the parking lot, walk up the steep Morning Sun Trail. At the top (**1**) start running to the right, downhill to the junction of four trails (**2**), and take Bobcat Trail straight ahead. Pass the trail to Hawk Campground and take Miwok Trail (**3**) counterclockwise around the FAA homing device for commercial aircraft. Stay on Miwok Trail to Bobcat Trail (**4**) and turn left. Follow Bobcat Trail back up to the four-way junction, turn right, and return to the beginning of Morning Sun Trail.

Alternative start/finish: From Fort Cronkhite parking area, run back along the road beside the lagoon, pick up Miwok Trail, and turn right onto Bobcat Trail.

Other Information:

Water and restrooms at Fort Cronkhite.

Be prepared for sudden weather changes, particularly fog. A hat, sunscreen, and jacket might all come in handy.

Telephone number: Marin Headlands Visitor Center, (**415)331-1540.**

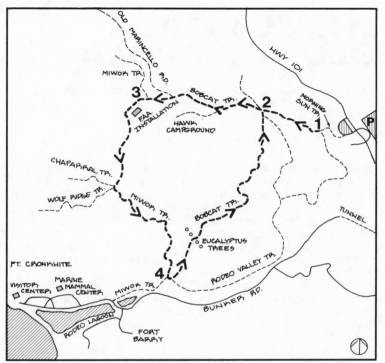

MT. TAMALPAIS OLD STAGE ROAD

Trail: *4 miles. Out-and-back; 2 miles easy uphill; 10% paved, 90% dirt trail; 20% shade. Views of the Bay Area.*

General Description:

Climbing to almost 2,600 feet above sea level, Mt. Tamalpais can be seen from every hilltop in the Bay Area, beckoning picnickers, hikers, and, of course, runners. Thousands flock to Mt. Tam every year to roam the two hundred miles of trails covering both the state park on her southern and western slopes and the Marin Municipal Water District land on her northern and eastern side.

Trails here vary from hilly single paths to wide fire trails graded to take the bite out of the mountain's slopes; most owe their existence to the Civilian Conservation Corps and the Tamalpais Conservation Club. These trails offer excellent views in all directions. To the west is the Pacific Ocean, with the Farallon Islands, twenty-five miles away, visible on clear days. To the east are the East Bay Hills, dominated by Mt. Diablo, and further still the Sierra Nevada range, visible only when the sky is perfectly clear. Also displayed are Angel Island, the Bay Bridge, Alcatraz, San Francisco, and the beaches along the Pacific coast.

Picking just one trail to recommend on Mt. Tam proved to be an impossible task for me. In fact I had a hard time narrowing it down to the four described here and in the next three runs. The ones chosen offer a variety of distances (from four miles to twelve and one-half miles) and degrees of difficulty.

The Old Stage Road is a perfect trail on which to experience the beauty of Mt. Tam and her surrounding landscape. From the Pantoll Ranger Station, a wide asphalt and dirt road climbs about 500 feet in two miles up the side of the mountain to the West Point Inn. The route was originally graded for the stage coach horses whose lot it was to pull passengers from Bolinas and Stinson Beach to "The World's Crookedest Railway," which came only as far west as the inn.

The well-surfaced, easy-to-follow path makes this a likely candidate for foul weather running, and if you are in the mood for a longer run, you can add mileage by continuing past the inn to the East Peak summit, two miles further.

Douglas firs, bays, and oaks grow on the mountain's middle slopes, but they offer little shade. More often the steep hillsides bordering the trail are covered with grasses, manzanita, chaparral, and scrub oak. Ocean and San Francisco Bay views appear far off to the right as you follow the curving hillside to West Point Inn.

Once the inn is reached, you have an exhilarating, almost effortless downhill back to the park headquarters. But before hurrying away, you might pause at the inn to read some of the literature posted on the outside walls which describe the mountain's rocks, trees, plants, animals, and history. You might also take a minute to savor the glorious southerly view of San Francisco and the Pacific Ocean.

After running, you can take a drive to the mountain's summit, where you will find parking and restroom facilities, a small visitor center, and a nature trail. The 360-degree views from the East Peak are surpassable only from an aircraft. For the truly adventurous, three hang glider takeoff sites are located near Ridgecrest Blvd., but only members of the Marin County Hang Gliding Association are permitted to use them. There are also year-round, tent-style campsites at the Pantoll (reservations available through Ticketron).

Directions to the Trail:

From Hwy 1 (Shoreline Hwy) north of Golden Gate Bridge, take Panoramic Hwy northward for five and one-half miles, following the signs to Mt. Tamalpais. Park in the Pantoll Park Hdqtrs. parking lot.

Alternative parking at Bootjack Picnic Area on the right one-quarter mile before Pantoll Park Hdqtrs.

Directions for the Run:

From Pantoll Park Hdqtrs., cross the road and take the paved Old Stage Road. Follow it uphill (dirt surface about one-half mile) to West Point Inn (1), turn around and return to Pantoll.

Other Information:

Water and restrooms at Pantoll Park Hdqtrs., West Point Inn, and Bootjack Picnic Area. Ranger usually on duty. Picnic tables; camp sites; hang gliding.

On hot summer days, area may be closed due to fire danger; call ranger station.

Telephone numbers: Pantoll Ranger Station, **(415)388-2070**; Mt. Tamalpais State Park (Admin.), **(415)456-1286**.

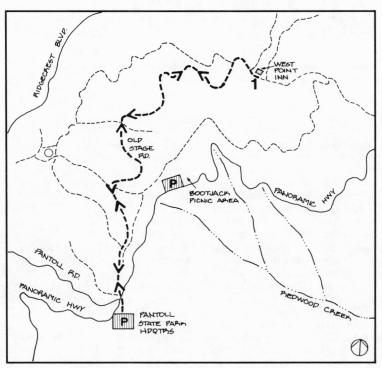

MT. TAMALPAIS MOUNTAIN THEATER

Trail: *4.5 miles. Loop; hilly; 95% dirt trails; 60% shade. Views of the Bay Area. Streams.*

General Description:

With its constant variations in surface, surroundings, and distant views, this run will undoubtedly appear shorter than it is.

The first leg of the run, Easy Grade Trail, true to its name, causes little hardship as it winds upward toward Mountain Theater. The trail is mostly shaded, but through occasional clearings you can see far away to the Richmond-San Rafael Bridge.

After just over a mile you arrive at the theater. Following the trail to the right, you have the unusual experience of running directly onto the 'stage' of this natural amphitheater. Looking up at the serpentine and peridotite rocks which provide seats for 5,000 springtime theater goers, you are tempted to do a "turn": a quick song, perhaps a dance.

After climbing the steps on the far side, you can pause at the water fountain and look back at this magnificent tree-shrouded structure built by the Civilian Conservation Corps in mid-1930s. Even before that time, around the turn of the century, local hiking clubs would put on shows here for their own amusement. Nowadays the procedure is less simple, and it falls upon the Mountain Play Association, a nonprofit organization, to see that things run smoothly.

On Rock Springs Trail, heading toward West Point Inn, you will probably notice the giant 'golf ball' structures which were once Mill Valley Air Force Base's radar. The military no longer operates here, but the Federal Aviation Administration still uses the canvas-covered domes. There was talk of building a convention center and a rotating restaurant on this site but good taste seems to have prevailed, and the current plan is to remove all buildings, except the domes, and restore the mountain top to its original wild state.

As you get closer to the West Point Inn, you'll have views of the bay and the Marin headlands. The shade trees have long since given way to short stubby trees with branches swept up to the sky; I can never remember their names, but I call them "broccoli trees" because they sort of resemble giant broccoli stems. After running away from the mountain on a promontory with steep sides, you will come to an easy series of switchbacks which will bring you to the inn. West Point Inn is private, operated by the West Point Inn Association. Technically you must be a member to stay overnight or partake of refreshments; however, nonmembers can also enjoy a little hospitality during summer weekends. In any event, there are water fountains for all to use, and by now that is probably your main concern.

On rainy days or when you are tired, you can take Old Stage Road back to the parking area (see pages 22-23). Otherwise pick up Nora Trail in front of the inn Although it is fairly well maintained, there are rocky and steep places that call for nimble footwork. Matt Davis Trail, named for an early trailmaker who lived on the mountain, provides a zany zig-zig course as you cross bridges, dodge in and out of streamside forests, and negotiate occasional stretches of flaking serpentine rock. The sights and sounds of the Panoramic Hwy below and to your left will let you know that you're only half a mile from the Pantoll Park Hdqtrs.

Directions to the Trail:

From Hwy 1 (Shoreline Hwy) north of Golden Gate Bridge, take Panoramic Hwy northward for five and one-half miles, following the signs to Mt. Tamalpais. Park in the Pantoll Park Hdqtrs. parking lot.

Alternative parking at Bootjack Picnic Area on the right one-quarter mile before Pantoll Park Hdqtrs.

Directions for the Run:

From Pantoll Park Hdqtrs., cross the road, pass the barrier, and start up paved Old Stage Road. Turn left onto Easy Grade Trail (1), and take it up to Mountain Theater (2). Cross the front of the theater and start climbing the steps on the other side. Half way up the steps, take a right by the water fountain onto Rock Springs Trail (3) and follow it all the way to West Point Inn (4). (After running away from the mountain on a promontory with steep sides, you will then turn back toward the mountain; on the way back, watch

out for an 18″ step downward.) In front of the inn (on the south side) pick up Nora Trail and take it downhill to the junction with Matt Davis Trail (5). Turn right, cross the wooden bridge, and follow Matt Davis Trail past Bootjack Picnic Area and back to the Pantoll.

Other Information:

Water and restrooms at Pantoll Park Hdqtrs., West Point Inn, and Bootjack Picnic Area. Water is also at the fountain halfway up the trail by the theater.

Telephone numbers: Pantoll Ranger Station, (415)388-2070; Mt. Tamalpais State Park (Admin.), (415)363-4020

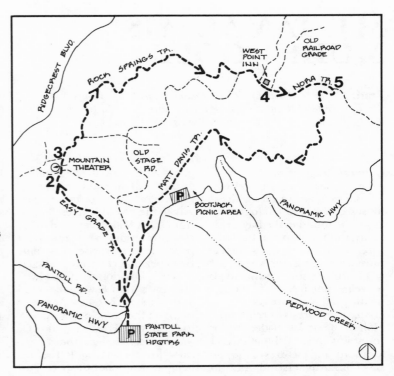

MT. TAMALPAIS MUIR WOODS

Trail: *12.6 miles. Loop; first 2 miles gradually uphill, last 3 miles steeply uphill, remainder downhill or flat; 90% wide dirt fire roads, 10% pavement; 50% shade. Views of the entire Bay Area and Pacific Ocean.*

General Description:

Of this run's twelve and one-half miles, nine are among the most scenic and easiest to cover of any to be found in the Bay Area. Sadly, this is not true of the last three and one-half miles. Scenic? Most certainly. Easy? No way!

The run is entirely on fire roads or well-maintained trails. It climbs gentle grades and drops into crisp, clean forests of redwood. Half of the trail is shaded, water fountains are available at several locations, and pictures of the East Bay Hills, Angel Island, Alcatraz, the Bay Bridge, and San Francisco flash before you. But after nine miles of glorious running, you are still three and one-half miles of difficult hill running away from your destination.

From the Pantoll Park Hdqtrs., the leisurely Old Stage Road takes you up to West Point Inn (see pages 22-23) and the beginning of the Old Railroad Grade (also known as "The Crookedest Railway in the World Grade." The train from Mill Valley used to climb this route to Mt. Tam's east peak.) Though shade comes only from periodic clusters of Douglas fir, compensation is offered by classic Mt. Tam views of the ocean and San Francisco Bay. At one point on the ever downward trip to Panoramic Hwy, a curtain of water is seen to seep from a vertical wall of rock to your left before being piped under the path. Further still, an old railroad platform acts as a reminder of the trail's original purpose.

After seven miles of running, you are in the midst of the first redwoods at the entrance to Muir Woods. You are running on a dirt fire trail through the trees, where only the sound of your own footsteps disturbs the silence. Several other trails branch off, but yours winds its way to the paved, level footpaths which signal an arrival in 'downtown' Muir Woods. But for the actions of conservationist William Kent, this area could well have been logged or flooded. He bought 300 acres here in 1905 and convinced Theodore Roosevelt to give the area national monument status. It's a tourist paradise, but a paradise nonetheless.

Turning left on the path, you run beside the fast-flowing Redwood Creek. In winter, salmon and steelhead fight their way through these waters to spawn. At this point, knowing that the 'hill' is yet to come, procrastination seems to be in order, and you might take a little time to read the informative signs posted throughout the woods. State-of-the-art procrastination would include a look around the visitor center. But that may be carrying things too far.

The uphill stretch will be familiar to runners of the infamous Dipsea race held each year between Mill Valley and Stinson Beach. Although you'll be taking a fire road rather than the narrow Dipsea Trail, the route goes up the same slopes, one of which bears the less-than-encouraging name of "Cardiac Hill." Easy to follow, the fire road just keeps climbing—sometimes steeply, sometimes gently, but always upward. For the most part you will be in the open, and the Marin headlands and Pacific Ocean off to your left, as well as a bird's-eye view of Muir Woods to your right, provide some comfort. A series of switchbacks and you're out in the open at twelve miles, rewarded by a magnificent view of San Francisco's skyscrapers peering back over the rolling headlands. Forking right at the top of a knoll, the trail disappears into the trees for the final leg back to the park hdqtrs.

Directions to the Trail:

From Hwy 1 (Shoreline Hwy) north of Golden Gate Bridge, take Panoramic Hwy northward for five and one-half miles, following the signs to Mt. Tamalpais. Park in the Pantoll Park Hdqtrs. parking lot.

Alternative parking at Bootjack Picnic Area on the right one-quarter mile before Pantoll Park Hdqtrs.

Directions for the Run:

From Pantoll Park Hdqtrs., cross the road and head up the paved Old Stage road to the West Point Inn (**1**). (The pavement gives way to a wide dirt trail after one-half mile.) Cross in front of the West Point Inn and take the Old Railroad Grade to the west, going downhill. When you come to a 'T' (**2**), go right and continue downhill, then gradually up past the barrier gate, the 5.3-mile mark, to Mountain Home (**3**). Cross the Panoramic Hwy into the paved parking area, continue beyond the far end of the lot, and make a hard right onto the paved service road (**4**). Follow the road downhill to Alice Eastwood Camp and take the fire road beginning at the barrier gate (**5**). Stay on the dirt trail all the way down to the paved path (**6**) and turn left beside Redwood Creek. Run through the redwoods past the visitor center and, keeping to the right of the parking lots, turn right at the road (**7**). Stay on the dirt path beside the road where possible, continue to the barrier gate on the right (**8**), marking the beginning of the Deer Park Fire Road, and take the trail upward. Climb steadily, for approximately two and one-half miles, (Dipsea Trail crosses the fire road several times) into the open at the top of the hill and fork right (**9**) toward Old Mine Trail. Follow Old Mine Trail, ignoring other trails, back to the ranger station.

Other Information:

Water and restrooms at Pantoll Park Hdqtrs., West Point Inn, Mountain Home, Alice Eastwood Camp (maybe), Muir Woods, and Bootjack Picnic Area.

Telephone numbers: Pantoll Ranger Station, (**415**)**388-2070**; Mt. Tamalpais State Park (Admin.), (**415**)**456-1286**.

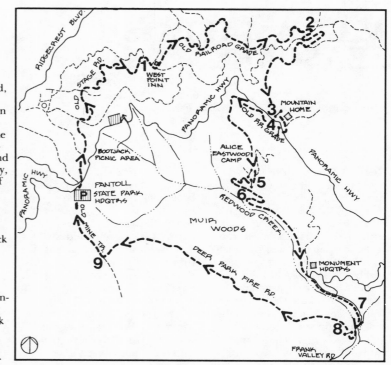

MT. TAMALPAIS SEASCAPE

Trail: *6 miles. Loop; rolling hills; dirt trails, rocky in places; 50% shade. Views of Stinson Beach, ocean, and San Francisco.*

General Description:

Heading west from above the ranger station, you follow the curves of the hillsides in and out of shaded woods of Douglas fir, bay laurel, and oaks. When you come to open grasslands, look to your left for views of the ocean and behind you for San Francisco's Mt. Sutro. Branching northward on the Coastal Trail, you can see Bolinas Bay and the sands of Stinson Beach reaching toward it. Roughly half a mile of running on the Coastal Trail brings you to the upturned wreck of an automobile, a bitter testament to the sharpness of "Ballou Curve" high above on Ridgecrest Blvd.

Where an unmarked but unmistakable fire trail (Willow Camp) crosses your path, you turn right onto it and encounter the only serious hill on this run. The good news is that you don't have to climb it all! After the first uphill stretch, you take the narrow path to the left of the hill before making a second, steeper ascent. Rather than running the first stretch, I would suggest walking backwards up the slope, enjoying a breather while casually taking in the spectacular sights.

The footpath brings you to Ridgecrest Blvd., and another wide fire trail takes you downhill into the shade of tree-lined Cataract Creek. Cataract Creek Trail follows the creek closely but is hard to see at times. As long as Cataract Creek is to your right, though, you are not lost, only briefly misplaced. Rocky sections, while not too difficult to run over, obscure the direction of the trail every once in a while, and caution must be used until, after one or two visits, the route becomes familiar to you. The many hikers along the trail should give you some sense of security, as well as verify the attraction of this area of the park.

After Rock Springs Parking Area and a short, steep hill, the trail forks and you head toward the Pantoll Park Hdqtrs. on Old Mine Trail. Old Mine Trail takes you directly toward San Francisco, which peers above the craggy hills of the Marin headlands. On a short downward section, look left to the Richmond-San Rafael Bridge and the sobering buildings of San Quentin Prison.

Returning to tree cover, the last leg of the run takes you along an often narrow switchback path down to the paved Old Stage Road, where you turn right and make the short trip back to the ranger station.

Directions to the Trail:

From Hwy 1 (Shoreline Hwy) north of Golden Gate Bridge, take Panoramic Hwy northward for five and one-half miles, following the signs to Mt. Tamalpais. Park in the Pantoll Park Hdqtrs. parking lot.

Alternative parking at Bootjack Picnic Area on the right one-quarter mile before Pantoll Park Hdqtrs.

Directions for the Run:

From Pantoll Park Hdqtrs., cross the road and take the narrow Matt Davis Trail west toward Stinson Beach. Turn right on Coastal Trail (**1**), follow it to Willow Camp Trail (**2**), and turn right. Climb the first short rise and bear left on the narrow trail to Ridgecrest Blvd. (**3**). Cross to the gate on the far side and go downhill on the fire road to Cataract Creek. (Note: At Cataract Creek a short-cut trail heads off to a footbridge, which is useful for crossing if the creek is running high.) Follow the creek north on the fire road and cross at the ford.

Make a U-turn opposite the water tanks onto Cataract Creek Trail (**4**). (If you're not carrying water, you might continue north to the Laurel Dell Picnic Area and its water fountains before making the U-turn to Cataract Creek Trail.) Stay close to the creek and follow the trail to the Rock Springs Parking Area (**5**). Cross the road and take the fire trail from the barrier gate to the top of a short hill. Then take the Old Mine Trail (**6**) marked "Pantoll" heading directly toward the San Francisco skyline, and follow it back.

Other Information:

Water and restrooms at Pantoll Park Hdqtrs.; water at Laurel Dell Picnic Area.

Telephone numbers: Pantoll Ranger Station, (**415**)**388-2070**; Mt. Tamalpais State Park (Admin.), (**415**)**456-1286**.

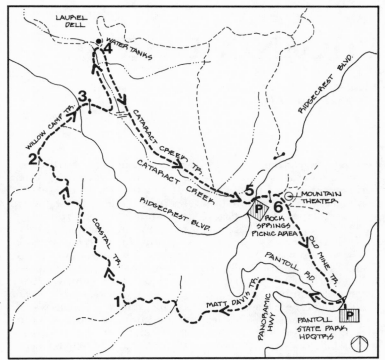

PHOENIX LAKE

Trail: *6.3 miles. Loop; hilly; dirt and some pavement; mostly shaded. Views of lake and wooded hillside.*

General Description:

There is an easy way to run the perimeter of Phoenix Lake . . . but this won't be it. The run outlined for Bon Tempe Lake (see pages 14-15), one of Phoenix Lake's four sister reservoirs, covers the less strenuous part of Marin County's water district lands, and so a more challenging course seems called for here. You could simply follow the relatively flat paths close to the shoreline, but the run described here involves several hills, one of which is particularly humbling. It also includes a section of trail whose continued existence seems to be in some doubt. Tucker Trail, as it is known, is a narrow roller-coaster ride through thickly wooded canyons, with obstacles including creeks, roots, and an odd rock or two thrown in for

good measure. It's a fun trail, but not one to attempt during or soon after bad weather. Because of narrow secluded paths with sharp drop-offs in places, a running partner is an added safeguard.

A wide fire trail climbs gradually above the picnic grounds to Phoenix Lake spillway. Emptied for repair during much of 1984, the lake is due to be refilled again by the winter of '85. This is a beautiful spot in the early morning when a fine mist rises from the water and sunlight filters in among the trees.

From here the run loops around the lake, climbing and descending on fire trails. You will enjoy an exhilarating reminder of childlike pleasures as you run through woods and leap across creeks—with periodic views of the canyon, lake, and Mt. Tamalpais.

The lake, sitting snugly at the base of Mt. Tamalpais' heavily wooded north side and surrounded by hills rising away from all its banks, is richly forested with redwood, Douglas fir, tan oak, bigleaf maple and alder. Looking north from the fire road near the water filtration plant, the entire valley is visible: the lake, tree-covered hills capped with scrub and grasses, and behind them, views of the San Pablo Bay and the Richmond-San Rafael Bridge.

After completing a trail like this, some refreshments might be in order. The nearby towns of San Anselmo, Ross, and Larkspur are full of eating and drinking establishments to suit all tastes and pockets. Alternatively, you can drive to Larkspur and board the ferry to San Francisco.

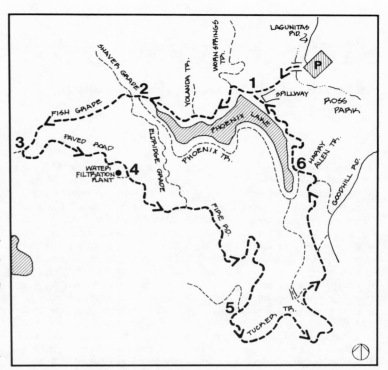

Directions to the Trail:

Take Sir Francis Drake Blvd. to the town of Ross and go west on Lagunitas Road to Ross Park. Park in the lot. (No parking is allowed on Lagunitas Road near the park.)

Directions for the Run:

From the parking lot, take the bridge across Ross Creek and climb the fire road to the spillway (1). Bear right along the north bank of the lake to the trail junction at the western tip, the 1-mile mark. Cross the creek on Fish Grade (2), climb one-half mile to the paved road (3), and turn left. Continue on pavement for one-half mile to the water filtration plant (4), the 2-mile mark. Go around the back of the plant and follow the fire road downhill, then uphill. Where the road forks, take either fork, as the two combine again after a few yards. (The left fork is longer but less taxing.) Soon after the trees open up, show-ing Mt. Tam, look out for Tucker Trail (5), marked "Phoenix Lake 1.5 miles." Take Tucker Trail to the left from a sharp turn in the fire road. The trail turns hard left in front of the first creekbed, winds down the hillside crossing several more creeks, then climbs upward. (The trail to Tucker Camp goes off to the left over a wooden bridge.) At the next two forks turn left, and at the fire road (6) turn right back to the spillway. Turn right again and retrace your steps to the finish.

Other Information:

Water and restrooms at start/finish. Picnic tables. Tucker Trail not recommended after wet weather.

Note: Hikers and horseback riders have priority on trails in this area.

Telephone number: Marin Municipal Water District, (415)924-4600.

STINSON BEACH

Trail: *4 miles. Out-and-back; flat; sand; exposed.*

General Description:

Stinson Beach is not really a place for a serious run, but then who said runnning had to be serious? Consider this a romp! Enjoy the novelty of running up to five miles on firm sand with frothy waves nipping at your feet, take in great gulps of sea air and work up an appetite, chase the gulls, gaze at the hillsides or survey the ocean for sailboats or whales.

Originally called Willow Camp, Stinson Beach has attracted visitors for over a hundred years. In the 1870s, Captain Alfred Easkoot rented out tents on the beach, and ten years later Nathan Stinson set up some competition. For years there were plans to extend the mountain railway from Mill Valley to service this region, but squatters, Mexican land grantees, and Nathan Stinson all laid claim to the land, and years of litigation quashed any hope of a railroad. Seadrift, the private property on the northern section of the beach, has been a source of dispute for three-quarters of a century.

Running here in the summer is like negotiating an obstacle course, weaving through frisbee throwers, would-be quarterbacks, volleyball players, and sandcastle engineers. But this can add to the fun if approached in a true 'beach spirit'. In winter—or early morning—the atmosphere is strikingly different. Only the hearty are present: beachcombers, their faces set in looks of perpetual expectation; fishermen silhouetted in classic poses against the horizon; and windsurfers losing the battle against goose bumps despite their wet suits. Gone are the bikinis, Bermuda shorts, and cut-off jeans, replaced by sweaters and hats to keep out the cold wind and dank fog. In high-traffic months the snack bar here does a brisk business, but in winter, when you really need something hot to drink, it's closed.

You can extend the run to five miles by running south one-half mile to the cliffs, frequented by local climbers, and back again.

The town of Stinson Beach, on Hwy 1, is one of those eclectic coastal gatherings of art galleries, surf shops, restaurants, bookstores, and craft exhibits, each, it seems, with a large, friendly dog dozing in the doorway. The population here is diverse, and a barroom conversation might range from current marketing strategies to "if we could only get back to the values of the sixties."

There's never a dull moment for an observant visitor to Stinson Beach, and when your running program—or your life for that matter—needs a dash of spice, this is a good place to come.

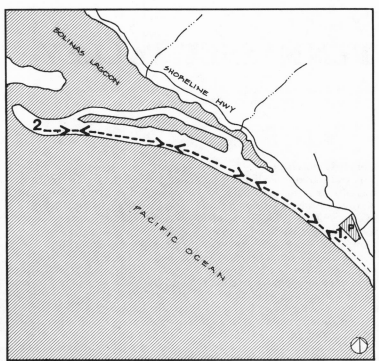

Directions to the Trail:

Take Hwy 1 (Shoreline Hwy) north of Golden Gate Bridge to Stinson Beach, turn into the Golden Gate National Recreation Area, and park in the large lot.

Directions for the Run:

From the parking lot, walk onto the beach and begin running at the lifeguard tower (1). Run northwest to the end of the beach (2) and return.

Other Information:

Water and restrooms at parking area. Stinson Beach Park is a day-use area, opening at 9:00 a.m. and closing one hour after sunset. It is advisable to check the tidetables and to run at low tide. The sand is soft at high tide, making for strenuous running.

Telephone number: Ranger station, (415)868-0942.

TENNESSEE VALLEY

Trail: *3.5 miles. Out-and-back; gently rolling; pavement and dirt; exposed. Views of hillside and ocean. Birds, horses, and cows.*

General Description:

If your childhood, like mine, included trips to the ocean, you no doubt remember the surge of excitement when you first sighted the crashing waves. For me, a run along Tennessee Valley, between gentle grass covered slopes to a small sandy cove, rekindles that kind of excitement. Especially attractive in spring, when the meadows of the valley floor and the hills above are blanketed with poppies, this peaceful setting attracts family picnickers, hikers, beachcombers, equestrians, and runners all year round. This short, relatively effortless run, which can be easily expanded by utilizing neighboring trails, has become one of the most popular running locations in Marin County.

Your run begins on a wide paved road angling gently downward. Soon the tree-lined Tennessee Valley Creek is beside you and Fox Trail, leading to Muir Woods, is off to the right. At the half-mile point the pavement terminates beside an attractive ranch and is replaced by a well-surfaced dirt road. Moderate ups and downs bring you to a fork in the trail: to the left, closely following the banks of the creek, is Tennessee Valley Trail proper; to the right the road continues. Both trails remain in full view of one another across the meadow until they again become a single path. Choosing the high road to the right will mean a slightly longer run and a more arduous climb, especially on the return trip. When it is dry you have a choice, but on wet days the creekside trail can be soggy and uncomfortable.

For this run we'll take the road to the right toward a private residence, the only one seen in the open meadow.

You will soon cross the Coastal Trail, a popular hiking route which, on another day, you could follow to Muir Beach, about three hard-earned miles to the northwest. Today, however, you go up the short, steep slope, then steadily downhill past the grazing cattle and back to the Tennessee Valley Trail. The creek quickly gives way to a large duck-inhabited pond and then a dam and spillway. The ocean is clearly visible now, and soon you are on the tiny wind-swept cove nestled between craggy cliffs.

It was here in 1853 that the Steamship Tennessee, looking for an entrance to San Francisco Bay, ran aground—fortunately without loss of life. The ship was destroyed, but its name was given to the cove and the surrounding valley.

The gradual 200 foot drop in elevation to the ocean must be climbed on the return trip but it is gained without too much difficulty, and the parking lot quickly comes into view.

There are few amenities in this park, although I did see a couple of picnic tables. Equestrians will find stables near the parking lot which are open to the public. Those with culinary inclinations can make the short trip to Mill Valley or Sausalito, where thirst and hunger can be abated. Another alternative is to wander over the hillside trails enjoying the ocean views, cool breezes, and wildflowers.

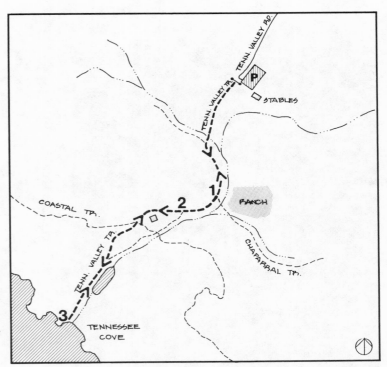

Directions to the Trail:

From Hwy 101 north of Sausalito, take Shoreline Hwy 1. Go left onto Tennessee Valley Road, follow it all the way to the end, and park in the lot.

Directions for the Run:

From the parking lot at the end of Tennessee Valley Road, pass through the barrier gate, take the paved road downhill, and continue past the ranch where the dirt trail begins (1). When the trail splits (2), stay on the wide road and follow it to Tennessee Cove (3). Turn around and return.

Other Information:

Portable toilets on route. Horse rentals.

It is advisable to bring water since the water source in Tennessee Valley is contaminated. The nearest drinking water is Tam Junction or Mill Valley. Also, Tennessee Valley is an important wildlife area—bobcats are frequently seen, and mountain lions are known to be in the area. Dogs are prohibited in the valley.

Telephone number: Park ranger (Marin Headlands), **(415)331-1540.**

Nimitz Way

CONTRA COSTA COUNTY

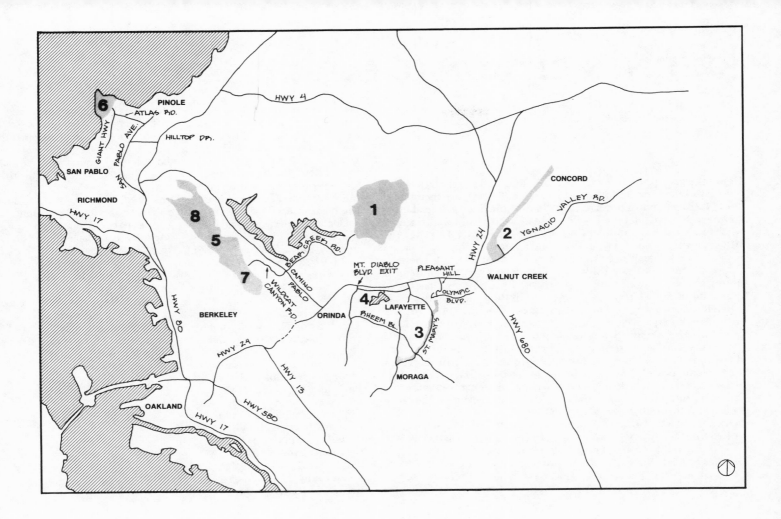

BRIONES REGIONAL PARK

Trail: *6.6 miles. Loop; very hilly; dirt; mostly exposed; can be windy or foggy. Panoramic views. Grassy hillsides.*

General Description:

What I know about ranching could be printed on a postage stamp with room left over for what I know about computers. But if I owned a ranch I would want it to look exactly like Briones Regional Park—wooded canyons hiding creeks and waterfalls, grassy hillsides, rich meadows, and a few ponds for good measure. Well, I may never own it, but I can certainly run through it.

The majority of the trails in Briones are only lightly used, allowing long, peaceful runs. There are several steep hills throughout the park, and unless you choose to run only through the meadows (which is not a bad idea) then one or two must be braved.

Running on dirt on the Old Briones Road Trail, you head gradually through a meadow, bordered to the left by terraced hills and to the right by a wooded canyon. Passing briefly under shade, you emerge into another meadow area and continue to a fence, with a corral on your right and a cattle loading ramp on your left. Cattle are plentiful here and have been since they were introduced by the Spanish back when most of the East Bay was a series of large ranchos. Indeed, it was the cattle, by way of seeds matted in their hair, who were responsible for introducing the annual grasses that now grow here. It's a responsibility that they seem able to cope with—every year the grass grows, and every year the cattle eat it.

Just before you turn left on the Briones Crest Trail the climb begins, first steeply, then easing up . . . but not much. You continue climbing for about half a mile, but the view of the hills rolling away to your left is worth the effort. Turning left at the junction with Table Top Trail, the worst hill is behind you and the route rises and falls gently. I would describe the views from various points along this ridge, but each time I've run here the fog has engulfed me. I do take solace in the eerie silence of the fog, though, and enjoy the sense of seclusion it creates.

A barbed wire fence joining you on the right denotes three miles of running. This is the Sindicich Lagoon area, and to your left is a cozy little pond, a popular picnic spot for hikers. Another pond is soon visible, below on the right, even through moderate fog.

Abrigo Valley Trail is my favorite stretch of trail in Briones Park, as it overlooks Abrigo Valley, one of the most serene settings imaginable—a combination of a meadow, green hills, a densely-wooded canyon, and a meandering creek. *That's* my ideal ranch!

Suddenly the trail narrows and becomes uneven for the short trip down to the valley floor. When you reach the sheltered creek, keep your eyes and ears open for the waterfall that can sometimes be observed. Soon the single path gives way to a wider trail for the final leg of your journey through the valley. No more difficult hills to worry about, only gradual grades to break up the run, passing in and out of shade and crossing streams.

Few facilities are provided within the park, so as to help maintain its unspoiled nature, but a simple picnic in a place like this is a true pleasure. More worldly delights may be found in Orinda or Lafayette only five or six miles away.

Directions to the Trail:

From Hwy 24 in Orinda, take Camino Pablo exit north to Bear Creek Road and turn right. Pass Briones Reservoir, and the park entrance is on the right beyond the Happy Valley Road turnoff.

Directions for the Run:

From the entrance gate (1), continue ahead until the pavement ends and go left on Old Briones Road Trail (2). Pass Black Oak Trail and a fence which marks 1 mile, and turn right at the junction with Valley Trail (3). A row of trees will mark 2 miles. Climb up the steep hill and turn left onto Briones Crest Trail (4) and left again at the junction with Table Top Trail (5). A barbed wire fence will denote

3 miles. At the junction with Old Briones Road Trail (6), go right, then left onto Briones Crest Trail again (7). Pass the lagoon and Mott Peak Trail, the 4-mile point, and turn left at the gate marking the start of Abrigo Valley Trail (8). Follow Abrigo Valley Trail all the way back to the paved road and turn left to the finish.

Other Information:

Toilets at start/finish; water and more toilets in the area to the left of the entrance gate. Picnic areas; archery range. Parking fee.

Telephone number: East Bay Regional Park District, (415)531-9300.

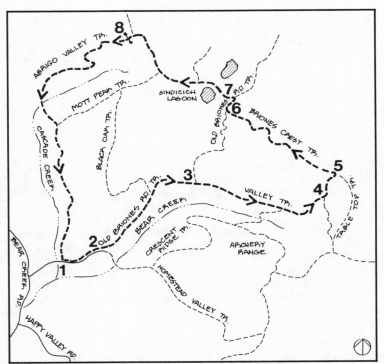

HEATHER FARMS PARK/ CONTRA COSTA CANAL

Trail: *6 miles. Out-and-back; flat; paved; mostly exposed. Residential area.*

General Description:

Walnut Creek has always been one of my favorite Bay Area cities, because of its friendly residents, clean streets, and great stores, restaurants, bars, and cultural activities. But I had never considered it as a place to run—that is not until I was introduced to the paved bike path that passes through the very heart of town. Operated by the East Bay Regional Park District, this trail makes its way past tract homes, shopping malls, supermarkets, and light industrial areas, and while not providing the most scenic of Bay Area runs, it allows easy running on a good surface. The route included here is only a small part of the Contra Costa Canal Regional Trail, which is U-shaped, dropping south from the Diablo College area, through Pleasant Hill, east across Walnut Creek, and then north to Concord, a total distance of just over twelve miles.

The trail described here was chosen because of its start/finish area, Heather Farms Park, rather than for any outstanding features of the trail itself. Heather Farms is an attractively landscaped recreation area with good parking, water fountains, restrooms, and many opportunities for enjoyment when the run is over.

From the parking lot adjacent to the Clarke Memorial Swim Center, you head north on the path to the left of the lagoon, where you can observe the antics of the local duck population. After leaving the lakes behind, you head east beside the concrete bed of the Contra Costa Canal, built in the late forties and still supplying water to meet some of the county's industrial, agricultural, and domestic needs. Your route is flat, paved, and fenced on both sides, and occasionally bordered by trees which only partially conceal the homes and shops pushing up against the trail. At about two miles a school running track, accessible from the trail, is off to the left, in case you feel an urge to do some intervals. Then you continue eastward, with a fine view of Mt. Diablo in the distance.

Since the return trip is a carbon copy of the outward leg, I tend to pay less attention to my surroundings on the way back and instead pass the time observing other trail users. There is a comfortable friendliness on this trail, and it seems to be a relatively safe place to run. You'll see as many bicyclists as runners. Fortunately the former tend to be of the 'easy pedal' variety, posing less threat to life and limb than the racers. A large number of walkers can also be seen cruising along at a brisk pace, waving hello or smiling encouragement.

For me, the most inviting post-run activity in the park—which offers picnic tables, an adventure playground, tennis courts, a par-course, and more—is a cool dip at the Clarke Memorial Swim Center. How do an Olympic-sized pool, showers, and heated changing rooms sound after a long run? The growing number of runners who are training for triathalons will also find Heather Farms Park a convenient spot to practice, since all three triathalon events can be pursued from one convenient location—slap bang in the middle of Walnut Creek.

Directions to the Trail:

From Hwy 680 in Walnut Creek, take Ygnacio Valley Road exit east to San Carlos Dr. and turn left. Follow San Carlos into Heather Farms Park, follow the signs to the swim center, and park.

Directions for the Run:

From the parking lot next to the swim center (1), take the trail to the left of the lagoon and pick up the EBRPD bike path (2) at the lagoon's north end. Cross the canal and turn right at Canal Trail (3). Follow the

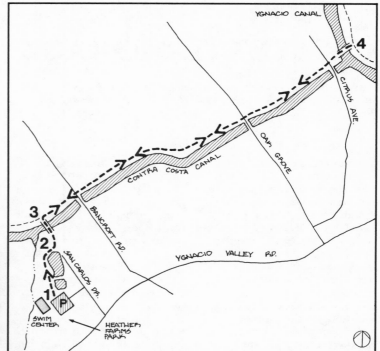

canal, crossing several city streets, to the 'T' junction (4) just after Citrus Ave. Turn around and retrace your steps to the finish.

Other Information:

Restrooms and water at start/finish. Swim center; picnic areas; tennis courts; snack bar.

Telephone numbers: Heather Farms Park, **(415)963-5859**; Clarke Memorial Swim Center, **(415) 943-5856**; East Bay Regional Park District, **(415)531-9300**; Contra Costa County Water District, **(415)674-8041**.

LAFAYETTE-MORAGA TRAIL

Trail: *11.5 miles. Out-and-back; gentle upward grade southbound, downhill northbound; paved; mostly shaded. Views of grassy hillsides and expensive homes.*

General Description:

It's a little hard to imagine that the Lafayette-Moraga Trail was once a railroad bed, part of the Sacramento-Northern system. Now it is a wide, flat, paved bike path, operated by the East Bay Regional Park District, which takes an uncomplicated route from the end of Olympic Blvd. in Lafayette to the Commons Park in Moraga. You can thank the forethought and the grading techniques of Sacramento-Northern for making the 400-foot gain in elevation along this six-mile stretch relatively painless.

After you leave behind the swimming pools, gazebos and barbecue pits of some of Lafayette's more elegant backyards, the environment along the trail becomes more rural. On either side of the path are apricot orchards, oak, maple, acacia, and eucalyptus trees, pasture land with grazing cattle, and occasional glimpses of Las Trampas Creek.

As you near Moraga, you will come upon St. Mary's College, situated on the far side of St. Mary's Road which the path parallels for some distance. It is well worth a minor detour to cross the road and explore the attractive campus. If your timing is right, you will hear the music which heralds hourly from the campus church's bell tower. The rolling hills in the distance make a fine setting for the Spanish-style buildings of this lovely college, which is now operated by Christian Brothers.

At the southern tip of your run is Commons Park, and although the trail does continue onward into the town of Moraga, this is where most runners turn around. It is a small, attractively landscaped recreation area, popular with family picnickers, and a good place to leave a second car if you are running with a friend and don't want to make the return trip on foot.

There are parcourses at either end of the run which can provide useful pre- or post-run stretching exercises. Lafayette and Moraga, both pleasant, easy-going towns, are worth exploring after the run, and both have an assortment of restaurants.

Directions to the Trail:

From Hwy 24 in Lafayette, take Pleasant Hill exit south to Olympic Blvd. and turn right. Follow Olympic until it ends at Reliez Station Road and park.

Directions for the Run:

From the end of Olympic Blvd. (**1**), follow the trail south (crossing many roads) to Commons Park (**2**), and return.

Note: For a 6-mile trip, turn around at the junction with St. Mary's Road. For a 9-miler, turn around at the junction with Rheem Blvd.

Other Information:

Restrooms and water at Commons Park.

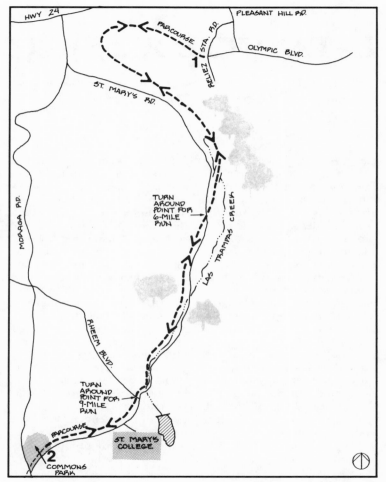

LAFAYETTE RESERVOIR

Trail: *2.8 miles. Loop; gently rolling; paved; some shade, mostly exposed. Views of reservoir and hillsides.*

General Description:

Within its 27,000-acre boundaries, the East Bay Municipal Utility District operates five reservoirs which collect runoff from hillsides and store water piped from the Sierras. The smallest of these, Lafayette Reservoir, has become a haven for runners: its pleasantly wavering asphalt perimeter trail encourages people to come and enjoy a casual run in the company of others.

Originally, Lafayette Reservoir was to be much larger and the water level was to have reached the top of the intake tower. But during the construction of the dam in the mid-twenties the earth moved, unsettling both the dam and the residents of Lafayette; consequently, the size of the lake was reduced and the tower rises high above the water's surface.

From the dam, you take the path downhill past the boathouse and park headquarters. On weekends this area is usually crowded, but an uphill stretch will soon put the crowds behind you.

One word of warning: this trail can get hot! It has little shade, the hillside is mostly brush and thistle, and the few willow and oak trees are too close to the water's edge to help much. In summer the steep-sided hills trap heat, and even the presence of the large body of water does little to cool off a thirsty runner.

As the run progresses, an occasional look at Mt. Diablo is possible, but for the most part it is the reservoir area itself that commands one's attention. At various intervals along the shoreline are fishing piers, where enthusiastic kids and stoic adults attempt to land black bass, catfish, and trout,

the latter having been stocked by the Department of Fish and Game. Also visible are adventurous boaters, maneuvering the various types of vessels which can be rented at the boathouse. Nestled among the trees beside the trail are secluded picnic areas.

From time to time other trails branch off to the right. These lead up to the notorious Rim Trail, a 5-mile hilltop run with sensational views and equally sensational hills. This dirt trail offers 360-degree vistas of the Bay Area at various places, but be prepared to climb up to 800 feet. If you should decide to give it a try, the option to return to the comfort of the perimeter trail via another connecting spur is always open.

All too soon the roller-coaster bike path swings westward past the Monterey pines which protect a large, group picnic ground, and

you reach the dam once more. Depending on what shape you're in, you might want to run the loop again. If not, how about taking a boat and just drifting sleepily on the water for a while? Since the reservoir is rarely used to supply the East Bay with water, the shoreline remains at a constant level, allowing plant and animal life, normally associated with lakes, to flourish. From a boat you can gaze at the groves of oak trees spared from submersion when plans for the reservoir were scaled down, and keep a lazy eye open for a deer or fox wandering the hillsides. With luck the boathouse snack bar will be open, or you can bring your own picnic supplies and stake claim to one of the picnic tables you saw on your travels.

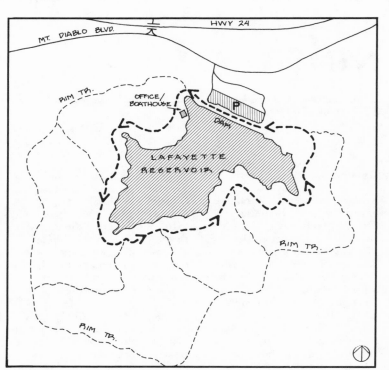

Directions to the Trail:

From Hwy 24 in Lafayette, take Mt. Diablo Blvd./Acalanes Road exit. Turn left onto Mt. Diablo Blvd. and follow it eastward, paralleling the freeway. The entrance to the reservoir is on the right. Drive up the hill and park on top of the dam or at the boathouse.

Directions for the Run:

From the top of the dam, take the paved bike path counterclockwise all the way around the reservoir until it returns to the dam.

Other Information:

Toilets and water at the boathouse. Picnic areas; fishing; snack bar. A parking fee is charged. To avoid it, you may choose to park on Mt. Diablo Blvd. and run up the steep entrance road to the dam.

Telephone number: East Bay Municipal Utility District, **(415)284-9669**.

NIMITZ WAY

Trail: *8.2 miles. Out-and-back; gently rolling; paved; mostly exposed. Views of hill ranges and reservoir.*

General Description:

The Nimitz Way (part of the Skyline National Trail route) is as easy a run as can be found in the East Bay Hills, yet it offers many of the same spectacular landscape views as the more arduous trails. Runners, hikers, and bicyclists flock to this leisurely rolling path atop the San Pablo Ridge above Berkeley. At times the Nimitz Way can be almost as busy as its namesake, the Nimitz Freeway, but on this Nimitz the commute is a pleasure rather than a chore: the trail is shared not with irate teethgnashers, but with relaxed runners, walkers, and cyclists enjoying their surroundings.

From Inspiration Point on Wildcat Canyon Road, the trail heads north into Tilden Park. Below to the left are the hills leading to the more manicured areas of Tilden, the most developed of the East Bay Regional Park District's charges. To the right are the grass-covered slopes descending to the blue waters of the San Pablo Reservoir. Passing occasional groves of pine, eucalyptus, and oak, the trail remains mostly exposed as it meanders through grasslands where sad-eyed cattle graze.

Wildcat Peak (1,250 feet) is off to the west near a grove of young giant sequoia trees planted by the Berkeley Rotary Club and the Park District in honor of persons contributing to world peace.

The paved trail terminates below the defunct and deserted Nike missile site. (The missile site is also approached from the north by the tougher Wildcat Canyon run. See pages 48-49). Having taken the time to run the four miles to this point, many runners will want to walk or run up the final few yards to enjoy the full-circle view of Alameda and Contra Costa counties before starting back.

Tilden Park offers many post-run activities. From Inspiration Point you can drive downhill to Lake Anza, where swimming is permitted between May and September. If golf is one of your sports, then try the nearby course, where you will also find a driving range and a practice green. For a more relaxing excursion, try a stroll through the Botanic Garden's fine collection of native plants. If you have kids running with you, the Nimitz Trail is a natural, because of its moderate terrain and the close proximity of other children's activities. Younger children love Tilden's pony rides and antique merry-go-round. And even if your older children hate to run, chances are that you can convince them to ride their bicycles alongside you while you put in your miles, especially if you mention the possibility of a steam train ride, which is another of Tilden's treats.

Directions to the Trail:

From Berkeley, take Shasta Road into Tilden Park. Turn right on Wildcat Canyon Road, following it to Inspiration Point, and park.

From Orinda, exit Hwy 24 north on Camino Pablo. Turn left on Wildcat Canyon Road, continue to Inspiration Point, and park.

Directions for the Run:

From the parking lot at Inspiration Point (1), take the paved trail west to the end of the pavement (2) below the old Nike missile site, and return.

Other Information:

Toilets at start/finish; toilets and water at botanic garden. Swimming; golf course; steam train; botanic garden; environmental center.

Telephone number: Tilden Park office, **(415)843-2137**; East Bay Regional Park District, **(415)531-9300**.

NIKE MISSILE SITE

HAVEY CANYON TR.

NIMITZ WAY

CONLON TR.

WILDCAT PEAK

PEACE GROVE

NIMITZ WAY

INSPIRATION POINT

WILDCAT CANYON RD.

POINT PINOLE REGIONAL SHORELINE

Trail: *4.5 miles. Loop; mostly flat with some rolling hills; paved and dirt; 50% shade; can be windy. Views of the bay, birds.*

General Description:

For most people, the mention of Richmond conjures up visions of sprawling industry and pollution. But just north of Richmond in Contra Costa's corner pocket is a veritable Shangri-La for runners. Point Pinole Regional Shoreline offers 2,147 acres that include gently rolling meadows, eucalyptus groves, salt marshes, and several miles of shoreline. A network of trails, paved and dirt, weaves through the entire area, and although there are hills, none are difficult to run.

Point Pinole owes both its name and its nearly virgin condition to quirks of fate. Early inhabitants, the Huchiun Indians, fed Spanish explorers a gruel called "pinole"; it must have been good gruel because the Spanish promptly named the area after it. And, improbable as it may sound, only the manufacture of gunpowder and nitroglycerine in the first half of this century by the Giant Powder Company and later by the Atlas Powder Company spared the land from the development to which the neighboring property was being subjected. Because of the sensitive nature of the product, it was manufactured in remote, sheltered locations around the point. The 'elbow room' that was provided for the explosives is now available to others for less dangerous pursuits.

The early stage of the run takes you north along Bay View Trail. True to its name, Bay View Trail offers a view of San Pablo Bay stretching away toward the Marin coast and Mt. Tamalpais. At two miles you come to a modern fishing pier. Its predecessor was the shipping point for the volatile explosives. As you turn inland, there are marshes to your left, a reminder of what the Bay Area was like before the advance of landfill and construction. After the shuttle bus turnaround point, you'll run through a dense stand of eucalyptus where it's cool and quiet. Eucalyptus are not usually planted this close to the ocean; however, these were intended to help contain any possible mishaps with the explosives. The remainder of the run takes you across a grassy meadow, past the green, tree-shaded lawns of the main picnic grounds, and across a bridge high above the railroad tracks.

Fishing from the pier is one possible pastime after the run; if you're tired, the shuttle bus can deposit you and your tackle there in no time. My preference is to just look around at the unusual sights, such as the remains of the narrow gauge railway, the half-buried bunkers in which the explosives were made, or the salt marshes with their abundant wildlife. Point Pinole has enough species of birds to bring on a case of 'ornithologist's eye,' and I strongly recommend that you bring binoculars and a list of the area's birds, which can be obtained by writing to the East Bay Regional Park District in Oakland. If you enjoy beachcombing, the shoreline has a wealth of 'stuff,' some worthy of investigation, some not.

Directions to the Trail:

From Interstate 80 north of San Pablo, take Hilltop exit west to San Pablo Ave. and turn right. Turn left on Atlas Road. The entrance to the park is on the right just after Atlas becomes Giant Hwy.

Directions for the Run:

From the parking lot, follow the pavement to the bridge over the railroad, cross it, and turn left on the other side (1) on the dirt trail going toward the bay. Turn right on Bay View Trail (2), follow it all the way to the fishing pier (3), and turn right again. At the shuttle bus turnaround point (4), turn left on Marsh Trail. At the fork (5), turn left and continue to Cooke's Point Trail (6), and turn right. (Ignore the first unmarked trail leaving Cooke's Point Trail to the left: it's a dead end, but you won't find that out until you've run a gauntlet of bees living in little white bee condos close to the trail.) Follow Cooke's Point Trail to the paved shuttle-bus road (7), turn left, and follow the trail back over the bridge to the parking lot.

Other Information:

Toilets and water at start/finish and on route. Picnic areas; fishing. Parking fee may be charged.

Telephone number: East Bay Regional Park District, **(415)531-9300**.

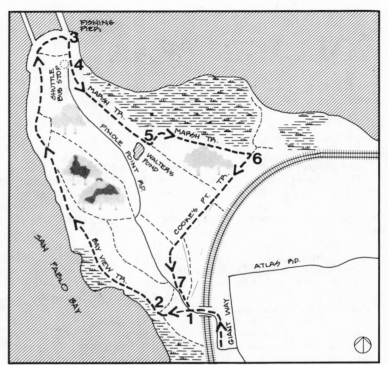

VOLLMER PEAK

Trail: *6.1 miles. Loop; very hilly; dirt trails, some pavement; mostly exposed. Views of San Francisco skyline, bay, and hill ranges.*

General Description:

The highest point in the East Bay Hills is Tilden Park's 1,913-foot Vollmer Peak. If you want to see the Bay Area from its summit, you can try your luck on the tough trail that leads you there. This run on the Vollmer Peak trails (part of the Skyline National Trail) begins and ends at Inspiration Point, as does the Nimitz Way (see pages 42-43), but unlike the Nimitz this path is arduous. Your route will climb through grasslands and small groves of eucalyptus and pine to the summit, downward toward the steam trains for a glorious view of San Francisco Bay, and finally through open meadows back to the road and the finish.

The first half of the journey is, for the most part, a difficult climb. After a brief jaunt down Wildcat Canyon Road, you follow Sea View Trail steeply upward, with Tilden Park's 18-hole golf course visible in the immediate foreground and San Francisco away in the distance. A welcome downhill stretch is soon followed by more uphill climbing. Along this trail are two alternative paths leading downward, in case you decide not to continue to the peak.

A paved service road takes you to the summit, with its imposing view of San Pablo Reservoir and the hills of Contra Costa beyond. Not only have you struggled upward for almost three miles, but you have done so with very little shade, which of course makes this run doubly difficult in the summer. On the way down, the service road takes you toward Tilden Park's famous steam trains, but the inviting sounds of people having fun remain in the background as you branch off of the service road.

A narrow footpath gives way to a wide, shaded dirt fire road which takes you steeply down into Big Springs Picnic Area. Your trek continues through open space until the trail forks again, and you take the downhill leg to the left. Enjoy this respite, because Wildcat Canyon Road is soon upon you, which means a final half-mile climb to the parking lot.

I would like to caution you about the dogs which are allowed to run unleashed between Wildcat Canyon Road and Vollmer Peak, a fact I became aware of only after coming face to face with a large Doberman (who fortunately turned out to be friendly).

Post-run activities at Tilden Park are endless and are described more fully in the section covering the Nimitz Way. For me, however, the only suitable pastime following a workout at Vollmer Peak is a long soak in a whirlpool—with the jets on full blast.

Directions to the Trail:

From Berkeley, take Shasta Road into Tilden Park, turn right on Wildcat Canyon Road, following it to Inspiration Point, and park.

From Orinda, leave Hwy 24 north on Camino Pablo. Turn left on Wildcat Canyon Road, continue to Inspiration Point, and park.

Directions for the Run:

From Inspiration Point, head west down Wildcat Canyon Road and turn left on Sea View Trail (1). At the junction with Big Springs Trail (2), the 2-mile mark, go to the left, staying on Sea View Trail. At the paved service road (3), go left to Vollmer Peak. Go past the tower and begin the downhill. Just after the barrier gate (4), turn

right on the dirt trail above the steam trains and service yard, and go downhill to the corner of the yard turning right onto the wide dirt trail (5). Pass Big Springs Picnic Area and take South Park Dr. until the dirt trail again branches off to the right (6). Almost immediately fork left at the junction with Big Springs Trail. When the trail forks again (7), go left to the road, turn right, and climb back up to Inspiration Point.

Other Information:

Toilets at start/finish. Golf course; steam train ride; swimming.

Telephone number: Tilden Park office, (415)843-2137; East Bay Regional Park District, (415)531-9300.

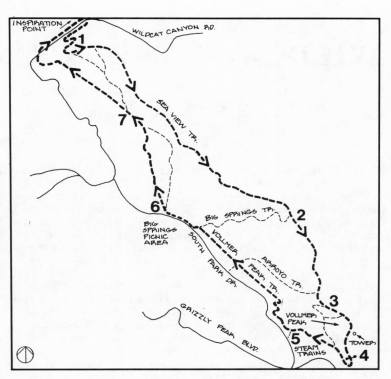

WILDCAT CANYON REGIONAL PARK

Trail: *10.7 miles. Loop; very hilly; mostly dirt, some pavement; exposed. Views of San Francisco, bay, and inland.*

General Description:

If you're in the mood for a hard workout high in the hills overlooking the bay and inland ranges, Wildcat Canyon is the place for you. Many miles of wide dirt trails roam the 2,200 hilly acres that comprise Wildcat Canyon Regional Park, providing great (but tough) running. Wildcat Canyon, unlike its neighbor, Tilden, is a rugged, undeveloped park, altered little from the days when dairy farmers once owned the land and supplied milk to the East Bay. Cattle still graze on the grassy slopes and seek shelter in the wooded arroyos.

Landslides are fairly common in this area, and because of them the run must begin some distance away from what was once the main parking area. The road is now blocked at the base of Wildcat Canyon Pkwy, and you have to run uphill past the slide damage and through the unused parking lot to the trailhead. From there the journey is almost entirely on dirt. The first stretch, alongside the creek that gives the canyon its name, is fairly easy going, but when you reach the Mezue (pronounced "Mez-way") Trail shortly after crossing a cattle grid, the long climb begins to the top of San Pablo Ridge. This is by far the most difficult section of the run, and in places you will almost certainly have to slow to a walk. You will observe that the hills about you are covered with annual grasses, artichoke thistles, and seasonal wildflowers; over your shoulder is San Pablo Bay.

At the ridge summit you can finally breathe easily again. From here the blue waters of the San Pablo Reservoir can be clearly seen to the east amidst the East Bay Municipal Utility District watershed lands. Coming in from the left is the Clarke-Boas Trail, the first leg of the infamous Skyline Trail, which is the site for the annual "Skyline 50," a tough fifty-kilometer race. Soon you meet up with the Nimitz Way (see pages 42-43), a paved bike path originating at Tilden Park's Inspiration Point some four miles to the southeast. For a 360-degree view, follow the short detour up to the deserted site of an old Nike missile installation. The Nimitz is a very popular running and cycling area, and you can expect company for a while. Continuing on the pavement, a gradual uphill brings you to where the trail forks, and you return to the largely untouched wilderness of Wildcat Canyon. Passing beside Wildcat Peak, the pavement gives way to packed dirt. Prepare yourself for breathtaking views of San Francisco and the bay.

From here on you might think its an easy downhill. You'd be half right—it is downhill. You're now on the Conlon Trail, which is as steep downward as the Mezue Trail was upward. If the opportunity to take your eyes off the trail presents itself, search the skies for a glimpse of hawks and turkey vultures hovering on the warm-air currents. Rejoining Wildcat Creek Trail, you can once again enjoy a relaxed run over moderate terrain until you reach the finish.

I have found no particular post-run activities here that I can recommend, but chances are you'll just want to go home and soak those tired muscles in a hot bath.

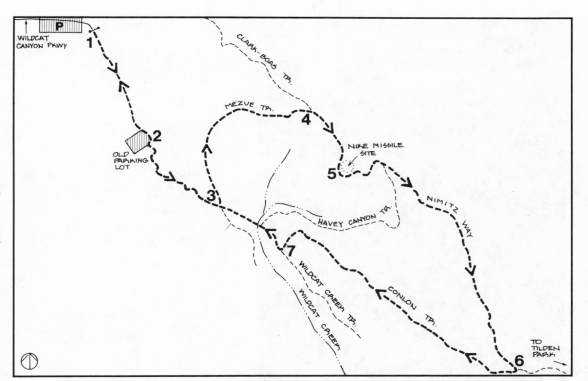

Directions to the Trail:

Traveling north on Hwy 80 in San Pablo, take Amador/Solano exit. Follow Amador north alongside the freeway to McBryde Ave. and turn right. Continue past the Alvarado Park entrance, bear left onto Wildcat Canyon Pkwy, and park near the barrier gate.

Traveling south on Hwy 80 take the McBryde Ave. exit in Richmond. Turn left onto McBryde. Continue past the Alvarado Park entrance, bear left onto Wildcat Canyon Pkwy, and park near the barrier gate.

Directions for the Run:

From the barrier gate (**1**), head up Wildcat Canyon Pkwy to the abandoned parking lot (**2**), and take the dirt trail from the far end. At the cattle grid (**3**), turn hard left up the steep Mezue Trail to Clarke-Boas Trail (**4**), and bear right along the ridge. The trail becomes paved at the beginning of Nimitz Way (**5**). Continue on Nimitz past Havey Canyon Trail (near some overhead wires) to Conlon Trail (**6**) and make a hard right up a short hill. Follow Conlon Trail steeply downhill to Wildcat Creek Trail (**7**), turn right, and follow the trail and parkway back to the parking lot.

Other Information:

There are no toilets or water in the park, and I recommend carrying water, especially in the summer months. Toilets and water at Alvarado park.

If you want to avoid the steep climb, instead of turning on Mezue Trail, continue through the valley on Wildcat Creek Trail for about three miles to Tilden Park. This route only climbs about 200 feet and is a very attractive alternative to the run described here.

Telephone number: East Bay Regional Park District, (**415**)**531-9300**.

ALAMEDA COUNTY

Hayward Regional Shoreline

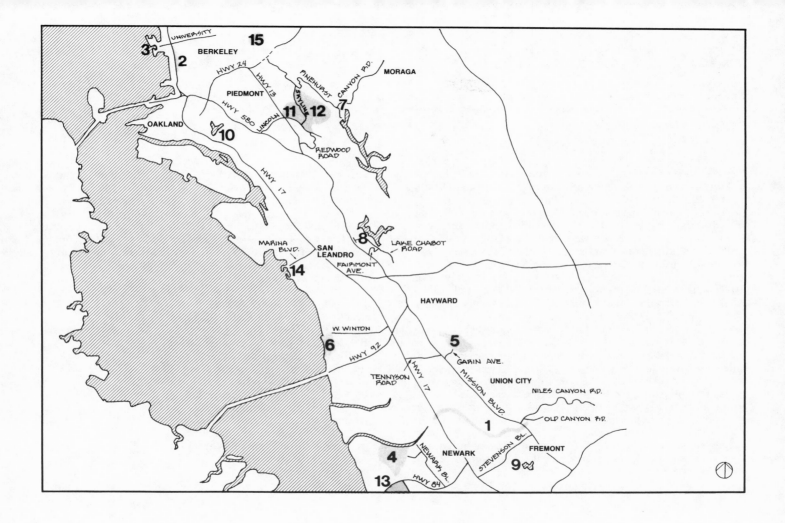

ALAMEDA CREEK REGIONAL TRAIL

Trail: *15.7 miles. Out-and-back; flat; paved bike path and equestrian trail; some shade; can be windy. Views of housing tract, lake, farm, and marsh. Creek.*

General Description:

The Alameda Creek Trail was built in 1973 by the U.S. Army Corps of Engineers in conjunction with the Alameda County Flood Control District. The project was the first of its kind in the East Bay, connecting various park areas and towns by a trail for recreational use. The trail parallels the wide Alameda Creek and its flood control channel all the way from the town of Niles, near Fremont, to Coyote Hills Regional Park and the San Francisco Bay some twelve miles away. Actually there are two trails: a paved bike path on the southern bank and a gravel equestrian trail along the northern bank. Those not inclined to make the 15.7-mile round trip suggested here are provided with several places to cross the creek and return via the equestrian trail.

Longer runs can be had by continuing to Coyote Hills Regional Park (see pages 58-59).

This trail offers the runner a variable-distance run over a flat, paved surface with a mixture of urban and rural scenery. With the grassy hills of Niles as a backdrop, you will pass underneath roads, freeway, railroad, and BART tracks, neatly avoiding traffic at all points. The landscape beside the trail changes frequently, from housing tracts to cabbage patches to water-filled gravel quarries to trailer parks. Numerous trees, including pine, pepper, acacia, and the ever-present eucalyptus line the route, offering little shade, but helping to break the frequent breezes coming in from the bay. The creek itself, some twenty feet below, provides a playground for adven-turous children and a feeding ground for pelicans, ducks, egrets, occasional swans, and other birds.

This isn't the prettiest run in the East Bay. Concrete and rock-work—the result of decades of "flood-control" engineering—line the creek banks, and the trail manages to shake off the trappings of civilization only when it reaches Coyote Hills Regional Park. On the other hand, it's a flat, long run without automobile traffic, and the mixture of homes, factories, farms, and more natural areas ensures that it is never boring.

Post-run activities might include a trip through nearby Niles, especially if you enjoy browsing in antique stores. Film buffs are no doubt already aware that Gloria Swanson, Charlie Chaplin, and other silent greats made movies here before heading south to help make Hollywood what it is today. One of the Bay Area's best, but little known "Fun Runs" is held here in June, combined with a crafts fair, music, and a Charlie Chaplin look-alike contest.

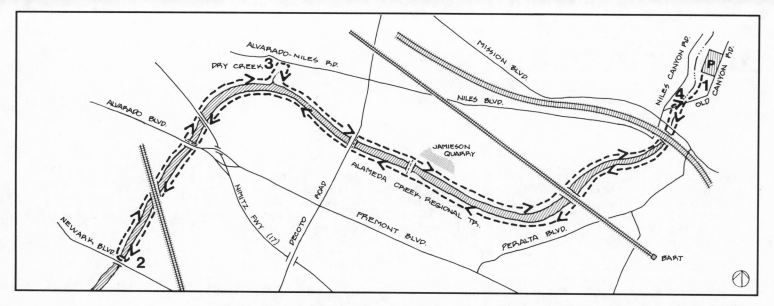

Directions to the Trail:

From Hwy 17 (Nimitz Fwy) in Newark, take Stevenson Blvd. east to Mission Blvd. and turn left. At Niles Canyon Road turn right, and right again onto Old Canyon Road, which crosses the creek. The parking lot is about 100 yards on the left.

Heading south on Hwy 17 in Hayward, take Alvarado-Niles Road east. Continue on Niles Blvd. to Niles Canyon Road and turn left. Turn right on Old Canyon Road and continue to the parking lot.

Directions for the Run:

From the gate at the west end of the parking lot (1), follow the trail 7.5 miles to Newark Blvd. (2). Cross the creek and return on the equestrian trail. At the 10-mile point you are required to make a half-mile detour to cross Dry Creek on Alvarado-Niles Road (3). Come back to Alameda Creek, following it for five miles before bearing right on Old Canyon Road (4). Cross the creek, turn left on the original trail, and return to the parking lot.

For a 5-mile run, cross the bridge which dead ends onto the equestrian trail at Jamieson Quarry and return.

For an 8.2-mile run, cross Alameda Creek at Decoto Road and return.

For a 13-mile run, cross on Alvarado Blvd. (just after the Nimitz Fwy overpass) and return.

Other Information:

Water and portable toilets at the start/finish and on route. Equestrians (north bank); cyclists.

The June Fun Run is a 10-kilometer run, mostly on Alameda Creek Trail, starting and finishing on Niles Blvd. To get to the town of Niles, take Mission Blvd. southeast to Niles Canyon Road, turn right and pass under the railroad to Niles Blvd., and turn right into town.

Telephone number: East Bay Regional Park District, **(415)531-9300**.

AQUATIC PARK

Trail: *2.5 miles. Loop; flat; mostly paved; some shade. Views of lake and freeway. Birds.*

General Description:

If you find yourself caught in commuter traffic on Hwy 17 in Berkeley, you might put your time to better use by pulling off the freeway and heading to Aquatic Park.

Sandwiched unceremoniously between Interstate 80 to the west and industrial buildings and railroad tracks to the east, Aquatic Park is actually a cigar-shaped saltwater lake with very little park in evidence. Despite its precarious location, created when the freeway construction cut it off from the bay, Aquatic Park offers much to see and do. Circling the lake is a parcourse, and shaded picnic grounds are found on the southeastern bank, as is an area seemingly allotted to an organized frisbee throwing game. But the park's main attraction is the lake itself. During your run you'll see rowers, water skiers, and windsurfers. Numerous other small sailing vessels can be rented here, and lessons are also available.

At the southern end of the lake is an unpretentious building which houses a branch of International Bird Rescue, specializing in the rehabilitation of seabirds injured by oil spills. They allow visitors but ask that you phone first.

Migrating birds and those simply seeking shelter from bad weather are often seen along the shores and seem not to be bothered by the nearness of the busy freeway which closely parallels the western bank of the lake. It is unlikely that you will be quite as oblivious to the traffic congestion, but you can take comfort in the fact that you're not in it. Having escaped the indignity of rush-hour traffic, a run around the lake can help smooth out the day's wrinkles and pave the way to a relaxed evening.

If you are still not ready to go home after the run and it's before 6 p.m., Takara Sake and Montali Winery, both on Addison near the entrance to the park, are open for tasting. There are several restaurants nearby, such as Brennans or Spengers, where you can stop for a drink, meal, or both.

Directions to the Trail:

From Interstate 80 (Hwy 17) in Berkeley, take the University Ave. exit. Turn right on 6th St., then right again on Addison Way. Continue on Addison to the park and park as near to the Seabird Sailing Center as is legally possible. (More parking areas are on the west side of the lake.)

Directions for the Run:

From the Seabird Sailing Center at the north end of the park (**1**), take the bike path clockwise around the lake. Pass the road between the lake and the small pond beyond it (**2**), and continue to the far end of the small pond (**3**). Turn right around the pond, and turn right again at the far side of the pond (**4**). Follow the road down the west side of the lake and around the northern tip, back to the sailing center.

Other Information:

Parcourse; windsurfing; sailing rentals and lessons; wine tasting. No parking fee.

Telephone number: City of Berkeley Recreation Dept., **(415)644-6530**.

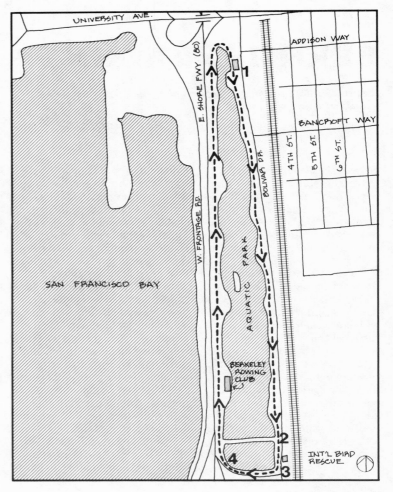

BERKELEY MARINA

Trail: *4.2 miles. Loop; flat; paved; exposed. Views of San Francisco Bay, yachts, houseboats, windsurfers.*

General Description:

Not far from city, industry, overgrown fields, and landfill, lies the Berkeley Marina with its neatly moored boats—a picture of composure amidst constant motion. Picnickers and wind-surfers mingle with ocean-going sailors and Sunday fishermen, business people rub elbows with merry-makers in the marina's res-taurants, and children compete with adults to see who's having the most fun.

The route begins at the south end of the marina, where scores of windsurfers, clad in wet suits, brave the cold of the bay. After you head west past a children's adventure playground, south be-tween the water and the parking lot of His Lordship's Restaurant, and then north along the water's edge, you reach the Berkeley Pier, which juts one-half mile into the bay. At one time it was over three miles long (derelict sections of it can still be seen). Because of the shallow waters of the area, such a long pier was necessary to reach water deep enough to allow the docking of larger boats. The San Francisco Ferry, established in 1927, used to dock here, and a train ran the length of the pier to bring passengers into Berkeley. With the completion of the Bay Bridge in 1936, the ferry was dis-continued and the pier fell into disrepair. The first half mile, which runs straight out into the bay, has been rebuilt and is now a popular fishing place equipped with restrooms, windbreaks, and fish-cleaning facilities.

Another extraordinary feature of this part of the run is a stun-ning and classic view of San Fran-cisco Bay—the kind of view people elsewhere see on post-cards. If the air is clear you can see, all at once, the Bay Bridge, Treasure Island, and San Fran-cisco off to your left, and slightly to your right the Golden Gate Bridge and Angel Island with Mt. Tamalpais watching over every-thing. It's guaranteed to take your breath away, no matter how long you may have lived here.

Soon after leaving the pier you head inland and skirt the marina, a modern, well-kept facility bordered to the west by restau-rant parking lots and small picnic areas. Strikingly peaceful when compared to the bustle of the pier, it is home to an impressive array of houseboats moored on the inland side.

The scenery on the return trip seems a little out of place. The bike path alongside Marina Blvd. is often overgrown, with weeds and tall grass, providing a sharp contrast to the well-maintained grounds seen in the early stages of the run.

Restaurants are an obvious consideration after the run. Many of the same views you saw while running can be enjoyed at your leisure from a restaurant window. You might also do some fishing off the pier.

Directions to the Trail:

From Interstate 80 (Hwy 17) coming from the north in Berkeley, take the University Ave. exit west. Stay on University and park in the first lot to your left after Marina Blvd.

Coming from the south take the Powell St. exit in Emeryville. Turn left at the stoplight and go under the freeway. Turn right at the next light (West Frontage Road) and continue to University Ave. Turn left on University and continue to the parking lot.

Directions for the Run:

From the west end of the parking lot (**1**), take the bike path past the playground and follow it near the water's edge to His Lordship's Restaurant (**2**). Turn right in front of its main entrance, and right again almost immediately. Run parallel to Seawall Dr., turning left at the pier (**3**). Run out to the end of the pier and back, and turn left again. Pass Skates Res-

taurant and make a U-turn at the Berkeley Yacht Club building (**4**). Follow the edge of the marina past the marina office to Marina Blvd. (**5**) and turn left. Pass the houseboats, turn left at Marriot's Restaurant and Hotel, and continue to the boat launch ramp (**6**). (This is the 3-mile point; you can retrace your steps for a 6-miler.) Keep going to the shoreline, then turn right, taking the gravel trail to the circular parking lot at the end of Spinnaker Way (**7**), and turn right again. When Spinnaker reaches Marina Blvd., cross the road to the bike path (**8**) and follow it back to University Ave. Cross University and return to the parking lot.

Other Information:

Water and restrooms on route. Fishing pier; restaurants.

Telephone number: City of Berkeley Marina Division, (**415**)**644-6371**.

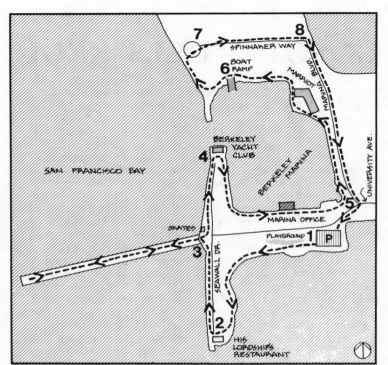

COYOTE HILLS REGIONAL PARK

Trail: *7.5 miles. Loop; 95% flat; mostly dirt, some pavement; exposed, windy at times. Bay views. Salt ponds, varied wildlife.*

General Description:

I must confess to having a soft spot for Coyote Hills. When I first felt comfortable enough with my running ability to venture away from my own neighborhood, it was to Coyote Hills I went, in search of a more interesting environment. And I found it. This quiet park with its marshes, gentle hills, bay views, and plentiful wildlife still figures strongly in my running program, and I never seem to tire of it.

Named for the coyotes who used to roam here, these low, grassy hills were once islands, but the nearby Alameda Creek relentlessly deposited silt at their feet until, after a few thousand years, acres of lush, freshwater marshlands were created along their eastern side. To the west are salt ponds separated by far-reaching levee walls, the San Francisco Bay stretching away beyond them.

A paved, fairly flat bike path some three and one-half miles long closely encircles the hills and provides a great introductory run. Since you won't need to be directed around that route, a longer run is described here which takes you through almost every feature of the park.

From the visitor center you immediately enter the freshwater marsh on a long boardwalk surrounded by cattails. Muskrats live here, as do numerous birds, whose presence is confirmed by bird watchers in almost equal numbers. Alaskan and Canadian ducks arrive in the late fall, no doubt relieved that the duck hunting club which once flourished here is no more. Where the dirt trail forks, you have an op-portunity to head off toward a few of the area's remaining Indian shell mounds. Ohlone Indians lived on this land for over 2,000 years, and the small shell mounds (refuse dumps for the Ohlone) and burial grounds are all that visibly remain of their culture. (For a tour of these shell mounds inquire at the visitor center.)

After taking a counterclockwise route around a grassy hill and picking up the bike path, the character of the park changes completely. Dropping down a slope to the pavement beside the Alameda Creek Flood Control Channel, you turn left and head out along the bay. You'll find no shelter from either wind or sun as you stray further from the hills. Completely flat, this path goes for two miles to the beginning of Shoreline Trail.

It's peaceful out here, following Shoreline Trail southward beside the salt ponds. Perhaps an occasional fisherman will nod a greeting. To the west is the Santa Cruz mountain range, stretching as far south as the eye can see. Often people fly kites and model aircraft from the hilltops, or sit peering through binoculars at sandpipers and egrets, or at a solitary runner out on the levee. Passing the levee that goes to the Dumbarton Bridge, you take Coyote Hills Trail to the bike path, which passes more marshes and then swings to the north, en route to the visitor center.

The visitor center is the best place to start post-run wanderings. It contains nature exhibits and a wealth of information on the Ohlone Indians. The staff are most helpful and can supply schedules for the naturalist programs they offer. Camera buffs, especially those equipped with telephoto or zoom lenses, can capture the antics of birds and animals—perhaps a red-winged blackbird, jackrabbit, red-tailed hawk, ground squirrel, marsh hawk, an occasional deer, or any of seven species of migrating ducks.

Directions to the Trail:

From Hwy 17 (Nimitz Fwy) southwest of Union City, take Dumbarton Bridge exit (Hwy 84) to Newark Blvd./Ardenwood Blvd. exit. Turn right and head northwest to Paseo Padre Parkway. Turn left and take first right at Commerce/Patterson Ranch Rd. and continue to visitor center.

Directions for the Run:

From the visitor center, cross the road to the bike path at the east end of the parking lot and turn left onto the boardwalk (**1**) leading out into the marshes. At the 'T' in the trail (**2**), turn left and then right at the base of the hill (**3**). Skirt the hill to the paved bike path (**4**) and turn right. After an incline, leave the bike path and take the short dirt trail leading down to Alameda Creek Regional Trail (**5**). Turn left onto Shoreline Trail (**6**), take it to Coyote Hills Trail (**7**). Follow Coyote Hills Trail back to the bike path (**8**). Veer right and follow the bike path back to the visitor center.

Other Information:

Water and portable toilets at start/finish. Parking fees. Levees periodically closed for maintenance.

Picnic grounds; kite and model aircraft flying; naturalist programs; Indian historic sites.

Alameda Creek, which flows along the northern boundary of the park, has bike and equestrian paths along its banks. These can be run as described on pages 52-53, or combined with the trails of Coyote Hills for some very serious mileage.

Telephone numbers: Coyote Hills Regional Park, (**415**)**471-4967**; East Bay Regional Park District, (**415**)**531-9300**.

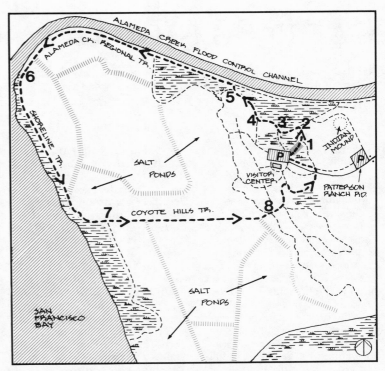

GARIN REGIONAL PARK

Trail: *7 miles. Loop; very hilly; packed dirt; some shade, mostly exposed; wide trails. Views of bay and hillsides. Pastureland, creek, and pond.*

General Description:

It may be hard to believe, but above the industrial areas of South Hayward are rolling ranchlands with pastures, wooded gullies, secret ponds, creeks, and 360-degree views of the Bay Area. Close inspection reveals deer, squirrels, and an abundance of cows endlessly chewing their cud. It's a peaceful scene, a reminder of what the East Bay Hills once looked like. The tentacles of housing tracts are slowly creeping up on the borders of this 2,000-acre island of protected land, and the ecology of the Hayward hills is rapidly changing. But here you can run high above it all and look inland at the splendor of the vast, still undeveloped Walpert Ridge in the distance.

From the parking lot at the end of Garin Ave., a multitude of dirt hiking and equestrian trails await the adventurous. Perhaps "industrious" would be a better word. With the exception of a leisurely loop around the meadow and pond, the trails here are tough. You don't get those bird's-eye views without a certain amount of wheezo-walking, and climbs of 600 to 1,300 feet await you. But the stout of heart and sound of limb will experience a most unusual and rewarding run atop the Hayward hills.

The run described here requires a steep climb in the early stages, then traverses the exposed ridge top before dropping (and I mean *dropping*) into the valley and following the shaded Dry Creek Trail back to the finish.

It's best to run here in the early morning when it's cool. I wouldn't recommend it on hot, smoggy days, when the rural charm and long-distance views are replaced by discomfort and a lack of visibility.

When you're through, you might want to relax in the shade near Jordan Pond, where you can also fish. Other park attractions are a collection of early farm equipment and a green lawn just right for barefoot walking. Or perhaps you'll just want to soak your feet in the creek and snooze for a while.

Directions to the Trail:

From Hwy 17 in Hayward, take Tennyson Road exit east. Turn right on Mission Blvd. Turn left at Garin Ave. and follow it uphill until it ends at the park.

Directions for the Run:

From the Red Barn (**1**), cross the meadow and take the steep trail uphill through the gate. Continue uphill through a second gate on High Ridge Trail, past a fork (**2**), the 1-mile mark, past the turn-off to Gossip Rock (**3**), steeply downhill to another fork (**4**), and go left. At the valley floor, the trail bears right to Tamarack Road (**5**), which is the 5-mile point. Pass through the gate and head north. Go over two bridges and through Meyer's Ranch (**6**) to the signpost on the right of the trail (**7**). Turn left opposite the signpost onto Dry Creek Trail, cross the creek and go left. Cross the creek twice more, pass through an iron gate (**8**), and continue to Jordan Pond. Take the trail on the right bank to the meadow and the Red Barn.

Other Information:

Water and restrooms at start/finish. Picnic areas. An entrance fee may be charged.

I would recommend carrying water on this run and wearing shoes with good traction. Also, don't run during or after a rain because of the difficulty of fording the creek.

Telephone numbers: Park ranger, (**415**)**582-2206**; East Bay Regional Park District, (**415**)**531-9300**.

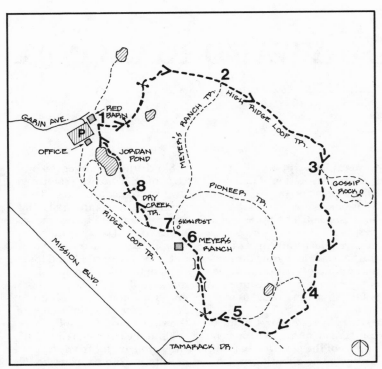

HAYWARD REGIONAL SHORELINE

Trail: *4.2 miles. Loops; flat; dirt; exposed. Bay views. Birds.*

General Description:

Once the location of numerous salt evaporation ponds, Hayward Shoreline is now part of the largest reclamation project on the west coast. Runners who come here regularly can enjoy a run on the flat trails alongside the bay and simultaneously witness the subtle changes in landscape and wildlife as nature reclaims the area.

Partially funded by Caltrans to compensate for the environmental impact of the new Dumbarton Bridge on neighboring wetlands, the shoreline is now operated by the East Bay Regional Park District. In 1979 and 1980, work began to remove sections of the levee system surrounding the salt ponds, and finally the levee holding back the San Francisco Bay was breached, allowing water to flow into the marshes once again.

Slowly the marsh vegetation is returning, along with some fugitives from the rare and endangered list: the clapper rail, song sparrow, and red-bellied harvest mouse. It will be some time, though, before all traces of the salt ponds are erased, and for the present the wide expanse of marsh and mud flats may appear empty and lonely to a city eye. However, as closer inspection of the varied birdlife that feeds around the bay's shoreline will show, you are far from alone.

Running often varies with the weather. The levee trails can be soggy underfoot following a rain, and sudden blustery winds can be a nuisance since there is no shelter whatsoever. However, when these same winds are reduced to a welcome breeze and the bay is free of clouds or smog, the resulting views of distant East Bay and Peninsula hillsides and surrounding marshes and mud flats combine to form a most agreeable setting for a solitary run.

Although at the time of this writing only a few miles of trail are in use, plans are under way to open more, and a recreation area will be built on top of the 'plateau' near the parking lot. Just before entering the parking lot, another trail can be seen heading north. This is the southern entrance to the four and one-half mile San Leandro Trail which can be followed all the way to the San Leandro Marina if you have a hankering to put in some extra miles.

If you're hungry after running, visit Manzella's Loft, a seafood restaurant that sits beside the busy Hayward Airport near the corner of West Winton and Hesperian. As you eat, you can watch many light aircraft take off and land. Another alternative, especially for those with children, is to take Hesperian north to Kennedy Park, which has picnic grounds, a petting zoo, and a small-gauge railway. It is also the start/finish point for the popular Hayward Half Marathon, held in October.

Directions to the Trail:

From Hwy 17 (Nimitz Fwy) in Hayward, take West Winton Ave. exit and follow it until it terminates at the park.

Directions for the Run:

Head south from the parking lot to the fork (1) and turn left toward the marsh. At the large interpretive sign (2) turn left for a few yards and then turn right. Proceed to a long boardwalk (3), cross the boardwalk, and turn right on the trail. Follow the path in a counterclockwise direction, crossing another boardwalk. Curve around to a gate (4) and turn left. Recross the first boardwalk (3) and retrace your steps to the interpretive sign (2). Turn left and run clockwise around the 'plateau'. After almost a complete circle, climb up the short path from the fork (1) to the top of the 'plateau', circle it in a counterclockwise direction, drop back down the same path and return to the parking lot.

Other Information:

Portable toilet at start/finish. Levees may be closed periodically for repair.

The main gate may be closed if you arrive in the early evening. Walk-ins are permitted, however, except during curfew hours (10 p.m. to 5 a.m.), and there is parking outside the gate.

Telephone number: East Bay Regional Park District, (415)531-9300.

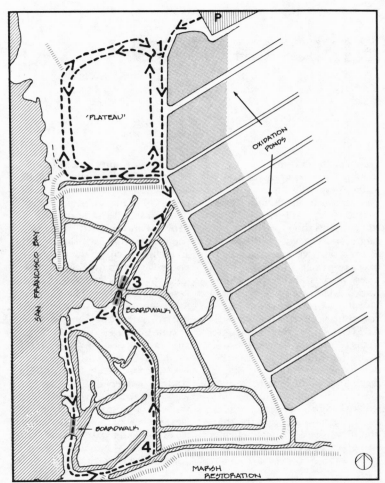

KING CANYON

Trail: *6.7 miles. Loop; hilly; dirt; mostly exposed. Views of pastures, hillsides, and reservoir.*

General Description:

King Canyon Loop Trail journeys through peaceful pastures and woods, and treats you to views of Moraga Valley to the east and the Upper San Leandro Reservoir to the west. Shared only with an occasional hiker or grazing animal, this well-maintained, wide dirt path climbs, falls, and winds for six and one-half miles of medium-to-hard running. Since this is part of EBMUD's watershed land, a permit is required, and you must sign in at the trailhead prior to departure from the Valle Vista Staging Area on Canyon Road.

From the parking lot, follow Rocky Ridge Trail, which leads to a narrow path through the shade of a pine forest. Cross the bridge and go straight on King Canyon Loop Trail. Soon you are passing farmhouses and climbing the steepest hill of the run. Happily, the climb is only three-tenths of a mile, and having conquered it, you can see the fine homes of Moraga and the rural expanse of the surrounding Moraga Valley stretching lazily to the east. Next you head down through the open pasture to the eastern tip of the reservoir and King Canyon. Swerving right at the base of the hill, you pass a large horse trough, and immediately after crossing a sheltered creek, you pass a tree farm on the left and continue westward into King Canyon. The trail is relatively flat here, and the waters of the reservoir are clearly visible. The signs of fluctuating water levels below testify to the reservoir's heavy use in the summer months. One of five reservoirs in the East Bay owned by EBMUD, Upper San Leandro Reservoir collects runoff from the surrounding hills and also stores much needed water which is piped from the Pardee Reservoir in the Sierras.

After three and one-half miles you turn north above the main body of the reservoir on a moderately hilly trail and follow the curves of the hillside. In the winter keep an eye open for flocks of wild geese feeding on the grassy hillsides or bobbing on the water's surface. Despite the presence of many oak trees bordering the trail, little shade is offered until at the five-mile mark you begin a descent through lofty bay trees into a meadow. Soon you'll rejoin the Rocky Ridge Trail and return through the pines to the parking lot.

If you are interested in a picnic after your run, head east on Canyon Road to Camino Pablo Road, turn right and follow it until it terminates at Moraga Park. There you will find water, toilets, and shaded picnic areas in a quiet setting. Continue on Canyon Road to the town of Moraga for a variety of restaurants, stores, and the busy Commons Park, another source of water, restrooms, and picnic tables.

Directions to the Trail:

From Moraga, take Canyon Road southwest to Valle Vista Staging Area.

From Skyline Blvd. in Oakland, take Pinehurst Road east to Canyon Road. Turn left and continue to Valle Vista Staging Area.

Directions for the Run:

From Valle Vista Staging Area (1) take Rocky Ridge Trail east and branch left through the gate and into the forest. Follow the trail near Canyon Road to a bridge (2), cross it, and continue on King Canyon Loop Trail to a gate. Pass through the gate and across the meadow to a fork in the trail (3). Take Rocky Ridge Trail to the left, going steeply uphill past Old Moraga Trail which heads off to

the east. Go downhill through open pasture to the fence at the eastern tip of the reservoir and turn right to the horse trough (4). Cross the creek beyond the horse trough and follow King Canyon Loop Trail, paralleling the fence into King Canyon. Stay on the trail all the way back to the fork in the meadow (3), and retrace your steps to the finish.

Other Information:

Portable toilet near start. East Bay Municipal Utility District permit required. Permits, which allow the holder to travel all EBMUD trails, can be obtained for $5 per year or $10 for three years from EBMUD offices.

Telephone number: EBMUD office: **(415)835-3000**.

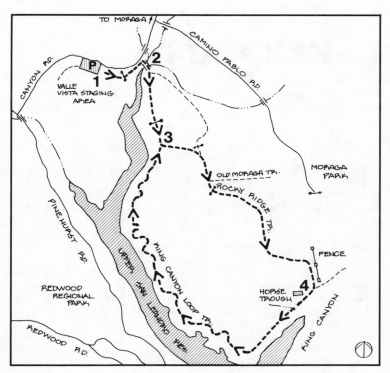

LAKE CHABOT

Trail: *7 miles. Out-and-back; rolling; paved; 50% shade. Views of lake and wooded hills.*

General Description:

Lake Chabot is a beautiful place to run. Owned by the East Bay Municipal Utility District, the lake is leased to East Bay Regional Parks for recreational use. It has fishing docks, boat rentals, a snack bar, picnic grounds, and miles of trails. Since Chabot is used only as a reserve water supply, its unfluctuating shoreline allows plant and animal life to enjoy a stable environment not found at other reservoirs where surface levels are constantly changing. The surrounding hills are covered with live oak, madrone, buckeye and wild grasses. The setting is picture perfect—ideal for a run.

Under good conditions, a trip around the entire lake is one of the best runs found anywhere. But the dirt trails on the north side of the lake can be tricky in bad weather or when they haven't been maintained in a while; I would only recommend running them with someone who knows the route. For this run, I've included the more commonly used western and eastern trails, saving the perimeter route for another day.

The usual place to begin and end a run at Lake Chabot is the marina. Heading west above the boats, you'll begin what will be a continuous series of moderate grades on a path mirroring but rising above the curves of the shoreline. Shade trees come and go, as do fishing piers, almost always in use below.

The dam soon comes into view; run across it to a spillway on the far side and then back again. When crossing the dam, consider what a monumental task it was to construct. Innovative hydraulic techniques learned from gold mining were used by engineer Anthony Chabot to wash earth down from the hillsides, with some 800 Chinese laborers doing the more conventional heavy work. Subsequent fill was trampled, layer after layer, by wild horses brought in from Oregon. These were crude methods by today's standards, but it must be remembered that this dam was constructed in 1874.

The east side of the lake is more popular with runners, perhaps because its grades are not quite so long as those to the west and brief dips into shaded gullies are a refreshing slap in the face. So be prepared to encounter more runners, as well as hikers and fishermen, on this leg of the trail. The lake is well stocked with trout, bass, carp, and catfish, and you will see people fishing everywhere—on piers, in tiny coves, and hanging out of rowboats. A California license is required, as well as an EBRPD permit, which can be obtained at the marina.

The return trip from the footbridge at the east end of the lake is a visual delight. Lake Chabot's blue water reflects the wooded hillsides climbing away on all sides, and in winter, fog over the lake often creates an air of mystery.

When you've finished running, you might join in the fishing or else rent a boat and explore such inviting areas as Bullfrog Landing, Raccoon Point, and Opossum Cove. Or you might just relax and have a picnic, often shared, of necessity, with belligerent ducks.

A group of runners of all fitness levels meets near the boathouse every Sunday at 9:00 a.m. for well-monitored fun running. Joining these informal sessions will help you familiarize yourself with the other trails in the area. (Also a note of warning—bicycle traffic is very heavy on the weekends.)

Directions to the Trail:

From Hwy 580 (MacArthur Fwy) in San Leandro, take Fairmont Ave. exit east until it becomes Lake Chabot Road, and the entrance to the park will be immediately on your left.

Directions for the Run:

From the snack bar at the marina (1), take Lakeview Trail on the west side of the lake to the dam. Cross the dam, turning around at the spillway which marks 1.6 miles (2). Retrace

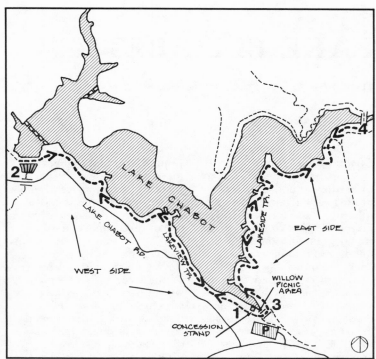

your steps to the marina, 3.2 miles, and turn left at the Willow Picnic Area. Cross the footbridge (3) to Lakeside Trail and turn left. Continue along the east side of the lake, past the barrier gate, the 5-mile mark, to the narrow footbridge (4). Turn around and retrace your steps to the marina.

Other Information:

Water and restrooms at start/finish; additional portable toilets on route. Boating, fishing (bait shop), picnic areas, horseshoe pits. Parking in lot (fee charged) or on Lake Chabot Road.

Telephone number: East Bay Regional Park District, **(415)531-9300**.

LAKE ELIZABETH

Trail: *2.1 miles. Loop; flat; paved; mostly exposed. Lake view.*

General Description:

A trip to the center of Fremont for a run may not sound too appealing at first, but consider the following. Lake Elizabeth (part of Fremont's flood control system) is a large, man-made lake in the middle of Fremont's Central Park, surrounded by green, shaded picnic areas to the south, broad expanses of playing fields to the north, and a marsh area to the southeast that figures strongly in lake expansion plans scheduled for 1986. The Diablo range, with its towering Mission Peak, stretches off to the east. And around the perimeter of the lake a runner will find a flat, paved path of just over two miles.

There are many other short footpaths throughout the park, but using them to add mileage requires constant changes in direction making it difficult to relax into a steady pace and enjoy the scenery. My preference is simply to run the lake perimeter two or three times to meet increased distance requirements and warm down by wandering through the play and picnic areas on the lesser trails. One such trail will take you to the attractively structured Fremont Civic Center building, which, when viewed from certain angles reminds me of the Starship Enterprise.

Other advantages of this jewel in the heart of Fremont are that it is only one-half mile south of BART and has an array of activities available after the run, including assorted boat and windsurf rentals, a swim lagoon, tennis courts, an adventure playground, a snack bar, and a public boat launch. There's even a library.

To my mind, the still beauty of Lake Elizabeth is best appreciated in the early morning or at dusk; the sights, sounds, and smells of water and land seem more intense then. But at any hour, the City of Fremont has a lake and park to be proud of.

Directions to the Trail:

From Hwy 17 (Nimitz Fwy) in Fremont, take Stevenson Blvd. east to Paseo Padre Pkwy and turn right. Take the first left and park in the lot to the right of the boat launching ramp.

Directions for the Run:

From the boathouse follow the perimeter path (in either direction) around the lake.

Alternative parking at swim lagoon off Paseo Padre Pkwy or at tennis and ballpark areas off Stevenson Blvd.

Other Information:

Water on route; restrooms at start/finish. Boating; windsurfing; fishing; picnic tables; swim lagoon; playing fields; snack bar; library.

Telephone numbers: City of Fremont Park and Recreation Dept. **(415)791-4320**; Boat Reservations, **(415)791-4340**; Swim lagoon, **(415) 791-4356**.

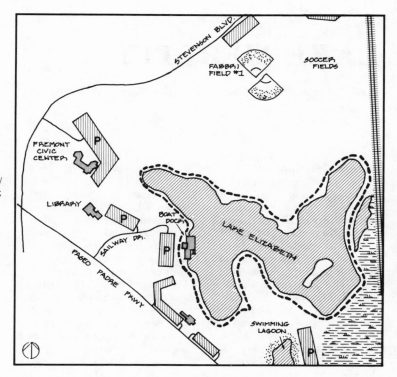

LAKE MERRITT

Trail: *3.2 miles. Loop; flat; pavement and dirt. Views of lake and city.*

General Description:

Visit Lake Merritt on any weekday at noon, stand on the path by the water, and wait—within thirty seconds a runner will almost certainly pass by. This lovely man-made saltwater lake in downtown Oakland is the most popular running spot in the East Bay—and for good reason: a view of Lake Merritt can take your breath away, especially early in the morning when the mist is lifting from the shimmering water.

The route around the lake is flat, paved, and full of surprises. The biggest surprise for me was finding such a beautiful spot in the center of a large city.

Located among Oakland's freeways and high-rises, a run around the perimeter of the lake will introduce you to a variety of intriguing sights and sounds: rowboats, windsurfers, a bird sanctuary, Children's Fairyland, Polynesian Gardens, assorted winos, a bandstand, the science museum, roller skaters, skate boarders, break dancers, drug dealers, bird watchers, drug users, cyclists, drug busters, walkers, dreamers, sleepers, lovers, and more. I believe that in poetic circles this place would be said to show "life's rich tapestry." Not being overly poetic myself, I'm more inclined to call it simply a great place to run.

Many of the Bay Area's most popular five- and ten-kilometer races are held here, usually starting near Lakeside Park on the north shore. It really doesn't matter much where on the lake you begin your run, however, and the availability of a parking space will probably make that decision for you. A convenient alternative to driving is provided by BART. The Lake Merritt and 19th Street stations are both within easy walking or jogging distance of the lake.

Despite its location in the heart of the big city, Lake Merritt is a relatively safe place to run during daylight hours because of the large number of runners using the path. It's still not a bad idea to run with a friend or two if possible. Unlike many other trails described in this book, the tremendous life and energy around the lake, not the solitude, are a prime attraction here.

There are plenty of places to visit after the run. The Oakland Museum is nearby on 10th St. and the 19th-century Camron-Stanford House is on Lakeside Dr. near the park headquarters. Open to the public on Wednesdays 11-4 and Sundays 1-5, the Camron-Stanford House contains a wealth of information about Oakland's past. If you want to eat, both Chinatown and Jack London Square, Oakland's restaurant meccas, are within striking distance. Oakland, long in the shadow of its neighbor city across the bay, has much to offer, and what better way to begin an exploratory visit than with a run around its handsome lake?

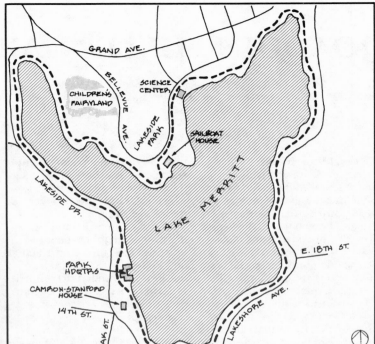

Directions to the Trail:

Heading north on Hwy 17 in Oakland, take Oak St. exit east to Lakeside Dr. and park wherever you can.

Heading south on Hwy 17, take the Broadway exit and parallel the freeway to Oak St. Turn left on Lakeside Dr. and park.

From 580 heading north, take Lakeshore Ave. exit, go west to the lake and park where you can.

From 580 heading south, take Grand Ave. exit, turn right on Grand and park.

Directions for the Run:

Park anywhere on the lake's perimeter and run either clockwise or counterclockwise around the lake, keeping close to the water's edge wherever possible.

Other Information:

Water and restrooms are near the science center. Museums, historical house, Children's Fairyland, Polynesian Gardens.

Telephone number: Park Headquarters, **(415)273-3092**.

JOAQUIN MILLER PARK

Trail: *3.5 miles. Loop; rolling; one short, steep uphill; shaded; dirt, short section of asphalt. Views of San Francisco and Oakland. Redwoods, creek.*

General Description:

Anyone with the name Cincinnatus Heine Miller has to be quite a character and Cincinnatus, better known as Joaquin, was surely that and much more. During his 72 years he rode for the Pony Express, lived with Indians, worked in mines, practiced law, and, as if that weren't enough, became a celebrity at the court of Queen Victoria due to his poetic work, *Songs of the Sierras*. In his mid-forties, this remarkable man bought eighty acres of steep-sided canyon land surrounding Palo Seco Creek in the Oakland hills, building several homes there and erecting monuments to his friends. A decade or so before, in the 1850s, the redwood forest which covered the hills had been logged, so Miller planted thousands of Monterey pine, eucalyptus, and cypress trees, which to-

day mingle with second-growth redwoods. These trees now shade the park's well-maintained trails which follow the creek and climb up toward Skyline Blvd.

Unfortunately, Joaquin Miller did not do anything about the hills, and any run over two and one-half miles requires at least one heavy workout. But these hills are also what attracts many runners who come here for some serious training over the tough trails that make up the annual Dick Houston Memorial Woodminster Run, a nine and a quarter mile lung-burster. Our run is far less ambitious, although it does have the inevitable hill. You can try it as an introduction to the park and use it as a base for exploratory runs on additional trails.

Starting near the Sequoia Arena gate at the east side of the park, you follow the paved road beside a lovely sequoia-shaded picnic area. The asphalt gives way to dirt and the Chaparral Trail soon becomes quite steep, but wooden 'steps' cut into the earth prevent you from reaching dangerous speeds. Less than a mile has been covered when you come to an opening from which Oakland and South San Francisco are clearly visible. A wooded canyon will be on your right.

After passing a stone bridge, the trail forks, and you take the Sunset Loop for a short uphill run past an attractive meadow and picnic grounds. The best is yet to come, but unfortunately you must first endure the worst—two short but steep sections of the trail that begin at the 1.5-mark. These only last for about one-fifth of a mile, though, and they bring you to the Sequoia-Bayview Trail, the best running in the park and perhaps the best of any described in this book.

As you begin to run the curves of this canyon trail, you almost immediately come to a clearing, and there before you, weather permitting, is a sensational view of Oakland and San Francisco. On those rare crystal-clear days, the scene appears almost too detailed to be real, as if painted by an artist. Returning to the trees, the path snakes along the hillside, remaining level, the trees echoing every footstep and voice, until after a mile you find yourself back at the Chaparral Trail. Circle the Sequoia Arena and follow the pavement back to Skyline.

The ranger station on Sanborn Dr. inside the park has a wealth of information about the area, and from there you can also easily visit Joaquin Miller's monuments, including the miniature castle he built for fellow poets Elizabeth and Robert Browning. Alternatively, you may wish to remain in the Sequoia Arena area and stroll the nature trail along which you ran ealier. Informative leaflets describing each numbered tree, bush, and plant can be found at the beginning of the trail or at the ranger station.

Directions to the Trail:

From the Warren Freeway (Hwy 13), take Joaquin Miller-Lincoln Ave. exit and go east on Joaquin Miller. Pass both entrances to the park and turn left on Skyline. Pass Roberts Park and park on the road near the sign for Sequoia Arena, 1.3 miles from Joaquin Miller Road.

Directions for the Run:

From the gate beside Skyline Blvd. (**1**), take the paved road to the right. Pass Horseshoe Picnic Area and restrooms to another gate (**2**), and turn right. The pavement gives way to dirt and becomes Chaparral Trail. Follow the trail steeply downward to the valley floor and turn left onto Sunset Loop Trail (**3**). Pass the stone bridge,

the 1-mile mark, continuing to the picnic grounds, restrooms, and water fountain at Greenwood Picnic Area (**4**). After a short, steep hill, turn left onto Sequoia-Bayview Trail (**5**), follow it back to Chaparral Trail (**6**), the 3-mile point, and turn right. Soon you turn right again up to Sequoia Arena and pick up the paved road on the far side (**7**). Go left at the fork and return to the finish.

Other Information:

Water and restrooms near start/ finish and on route. Historic landmarks; picnic areas.

Telephone number: Park ranger, (**415**)**531-2205**.

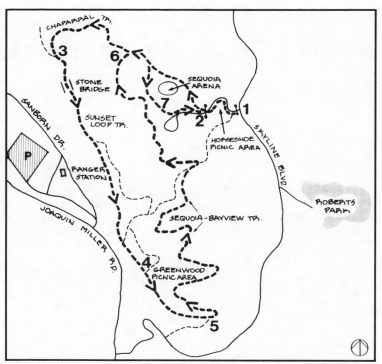

REDWOOD REGIONAL PARK˙

Trail: *6.5 miles. Loop; some hills (Canyon Trail is steep); mostly dirt, some pavement; 50% shade. Hillside views. Woods and stream.*

General Description:

Of the many fine parks operated by the East Bay Regional Park District, few offer as great a variety of trails as Redwood Regional Park in the hills above Oakland. This 2,200-acre park combines heavily-used picnic areas with lightly-travelled hiking and equestrian trails. The challenge of these trails is quickly apparent to anyone attempting to run more than four miles: beyond that distance, a steep climb or two is unavoidable. The beauty of this park lies in its redwood-shaded canyons and its exposed ridge trails displaying bay vistas to the west and vast expanses of hills and more canyons to the east. Deer, raccoons, and jack rabbits can often be sighted in the early morning or near dusk.

Once the most resplendent giant redwoods to be found anywhere in the world graced the hillsides here. Some trees were so tall that mariners used them as navigational bearings when sailing into the bay. The entire forest was logged shortly after the Gold Rush, and its timber used to build the fast-growing Bay Area cities of San Francisco and Oakland. Today a new growth of redwoods covers much of the park. Not so tall or wide of girth as their ancestors, these young trees are nevertheless proud and pleasing to a runner passing beneath them.

Of the many possible trail selections here, I chose one which gives an overall feel for the park. It is fifty percent shaded and provides a good base for exploring other possible routes. Another advantage is that it covers the toughest hill early, letting you enjoy the balance of the trail without strenuous exertion.

From the Canyon Picnic Area you take the steep Canyon Trail for one-half mile up to the undulating East Ridge Trail. Down to your right you'll see Orinda and Moraga. East Ridge Trail has little shade but offers quality running to Skyline Trail, three and one-half miles to the north. There you pick up Stream Trail to begin the second half of the run. After an initial downhill jaunt through eucalyptus trees, the trail levels off and you find yourself running almost silently on a soft quilt of needles, courtesy of the redwoods which are now shielding you from sun and wind. This quiet, secluded section of the run continues for about two miles before it emerges into the more heavily-used open space areas and brings you back to the parking lot.

After the run, you might visit the Huckleberry Botanic Regional Preserve on Skyline Blvd. A stroll on Huckleberry's self-guided path is a welcome change of pace and will introduce you to many varieties of East Bay plant life. A free brochure is available at the trailhead. Another welcome pastime in summer months is a swim at Roberts Recreation Area, also on Skyline Blvd. There is a fee, and it might be a good idea to check with park authorities about the hours the pool is open.

Directions to the Trail:

From Hwy 13 (Warren Fwy), take Redwood Road-Carson St. exit east. Follow Redwood and go about three miles to the main park entrance.

To begin the run at Skyline Gate, take Joaquin Miller Road exit from Hwy 13 to Skyline, turn left, and continue to Skyline Gate parking lot.

Directions for the Run:

From Canyon Picnic Area take the trail north to the fork (1), go right on the steep Canyon Trail to East Ridge Trail (2) and turn left. Follow East Ridge Trail to Skyline Gate (3), the 3.5-mile mark. Pass in front of the parking lot, then turn left on Stream Trail and follow it all the way back to the parking lot.

Other Information:

Water and restrooms at start/finish and at parking lot at Skyline Gate. Picnic grounds. Parking fee weekends and during summer if the run is begun at the Redwood Road end; no fee if begun at Skyline Gate.

Telephone number: East Bay Regional Park District, (415)531-9300.

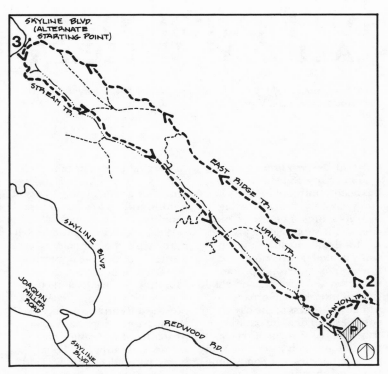

SAN FRANCISCO NATIONAL WILDLIFE REFUGE

Trail: *5.6 miles. Loop; flat; dirt trail; exposed, sometimes windy; not good for running after rain. Views of bay, salt ponds, birds.*

General Description:

For centuries San Francisco Bay has been a source of food, shelter, and recreation for those living near its shores. These days, of course, the supermarket provides the food and our shelter is centrally heated. Recreational use, however, is increasing, prompted in part by various environmental groups interested in broadening public awareness of the bay's complex and delicate nature. Running is one form of recreation not normally associated with the salt marshes, salt ponds, mud flats, and choppy waters that make up the bay, but in fact there are many miles of trails following the twists and turns of the levees which snake out into the water. There is not the merest hint of a hill on these levees. The bay breezes (perhaps a little too "breezy" at times), uncanny solitude, good running surface (except after a rain), and a variety of wildlife add up to some first-class running.

What makes this run at the San Francisco Bay National Wildlife Refuge special is the opportunity to learn so much about the surroundings in an easy and enjoyable way. The refuge, located beside the toll entrance to the "Old" Dumbarton Bridge has a most informative visitor center under whose roof numerous books, maps, pamphlets, exhibits, and friendly personnel can be found.

You are unlikely to encounter another person on this run, so if solitude is your desire, this is a good spot to choose. Threading your way between the salt ponds where many water birds feed and rest, nothing obscures your view of the Peninsula cities and hillsides and the South Bay—unless it is foggy. Surrounded by so many population centers, you may find the absence of city noises surprising. But these surroundings are anything but silent. Some 250 species of birds either live or vacation here, and many will be monitoring your progress, some protesting the intrusion with raucous calls which, if translated into English, would surely not be printable. Should your ornithological interest be sparked, you can pick up some literature in the visitor center which will help you to identify the more commonly seen birds, such as the least sandpiper, avocet, shoveler, and, with luck, the brown pelican.

The least interesting section of this run, on the far side of the ponds, parallels a railroad track and seems to be taking you to a large, smoky factory. The trail is often coated with a layer of salt crystals which crunch under foot and prompt thoughts of drinking water. Indeed, in summer I usually carry a water bottle, as well as sun screen and a hat. But easterly breezes, which often sweep off the water giving you a friendly nudge from the back, redeem this one and a half mile leg.

Once back at the visitor center, you can "warm down" by jogging or walking the Tidelands Trail. It is one and one-third miles long, and is dotted with numbered exhibits explaining many of the mysteries of the bay. Patience and a pair of binoculars will help in observing wildlife too shy to show themselves during your run.

Directions to the Trail:

From Hwy 84 southwest of Union City, take Thornton Ave. exit and follow the signs to the National Wildlife Refuge.

Directions for the Run:

From the west end of the parking lot, take the footpath down to the boardwalk (**1**). Cross the boardwalk over Newark Slough and turn right onto the Newark Slough Trail. Follow it as it parallels Hwy 84 and then turns south (**2**) for one mile, then east (**3**). At the first gate (**4**) turn left. At the second gate (**5**) turn left again, passing a second boardwalk (**6**) and returning to the first one. Retrace your steps to the parking lot.

Other Information:

Water and restrooms at visitor center. During the summer, it is a good idea to carry water, sun screen and hat.

Telephone number: San Francisco National Wildlife Refuge, **(415)792-0222**.

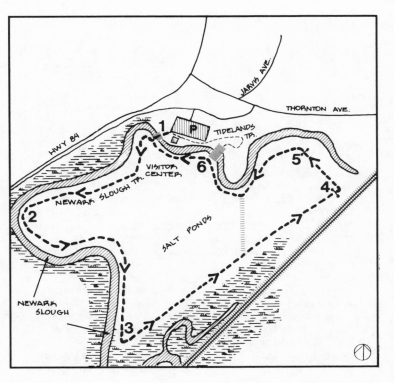

SAN LEANDRO MARINA

Trail: *6.2 miles. Out-and-back with loop; flat; paved and dirt; exposed, can be windy. Views of the bay and cities, Peninsula and East Bay Hills.*

General Description:

This run is a combination of three distinctly different areas: a busy family park, a parcourse, and a lonely shoreline. Together they add up to 6.2 miles of easy running in attractive surroundings only a few minutes from a freeway.

The run begins in San Leandro's Marina Park, site of the very popular San Leandro Shoreline Run held in June. The park's well-kept lawns and occasional shade trees are strikingly luxurious when compared to the dry grasses surrounding the parcourse loop which is sandwiched between the bay and a small lagoon. The newly paved shoreline trail takes you south, away from the throngs of picnickers, along the water's edge: it first passes close to a golf course, and then into a large expanse of wasteland stretching toward a row of mobile homes far off to the east. This trail, built on new landfill, will eventually reach south to Fremont, and already it is possible to follow it about four and one-half miles to the Hayward Shoreline (see pages 62-63).

Both the parcourse and shoreline trails provide splendid views of the bay, San Francisco's skyline, the Peninsula, and East Bay Hills. The trade-off is exposure to the often strong breezes from the bay. A wide variety of birds are seen along the shore, and high above, their metallic counterparts approach Oakland International Airport.

If you are fortunate enough to own a boat, there are good launching facilities at the marina. If you don't own a boat, the golf courses across the street could provide some solace. Those with children can turn them loose on the adventure playgrounds which offer some unique climbing and swinging challenges.

The Blue Dolphin, El Torito, and Horatio's restaurants are nearby for the hungry. Barbecue and picnic areas are also plentiful, though heavily used. It may take a little adjustment on your part to return to the group areas after a peaceful run along the water's edge.

Directions to the Trail:

From Hwy 17 (Nimitz Fwy) in San Leandro, take the Marina Blvd. exit. Follow Marina until it runs into Neptune Dr. Go south to Marina Park and park in the first lot just past Fairway Dr.

Directions for the Run:

Exit the west end of the Marina Park parking lot, near the restrooms (1), and follow the bike path to the beginning of the parcourse (2). Run the route of the parcourse back to where it started, then turn right on the bike path. Take the bike path to the bridge (3), cross it, and follow the paved trail between the golf course and the bay. Approximately one and one-half miles after the bridge, turn left (4); bear right at the fork under the powerlines (5). Go right passing under the powerlines a second time. Veer left at the fork (6) and head south toward the tall building in the trees. Run to the bridge (7), turn around and retrace your steps back to the first bridge (3). Follow Neptune Dr. bike path back to the parking lot.

Other Information:

Water and restrooms at start/finish. Picnic areas; parcourse; windsurfing; yachts; restaurants; adventure playground; golf course; boat launch.

Telephone number: San Leandro Recreation Dept., (415)577-3462.

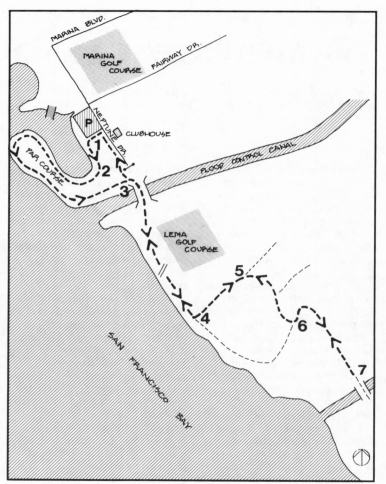

STRAWBERRY CANYON

Trail: *7 miles. Out-and-back; first half gradual uphill with one short very steep section; 50% shade. Views of Berkeley and San Francisco.*

General Description:

Probably the most popular run of its kind in Berkeley, this out-and-back trail takes you up and around wooded Strawberry Canyon above the University of California and provides one of the most stunning Bay Area panoramas imaginable.

From the small parking lot on Centennial Dr. you cross Strawberry Creek and gradually climb the pine-shaded dirt trail. After about a mile, a sundial beside the trail marks a sharp left turn, followed by a steep climb of about one-fifth of a mile. With this challenge behind you, you can relax and enjoy the rest of the run. The trail continues to gradually gain elevation as you leave the shade and make a counterclockwise curve across the face of the canyon. Many of the build-

ing you will see below belong to the university's atomic energy project, including the unusual-looking cyclotron with its eye-catching domed roof dominating the scene. A little further into the run the vista expands to include much of the city of Berkeley, with the bay and San Francisco beyond.

This spectacular scene remains visible until you pass between tall eucalyptus tress and near the end of the trail. Mileage marker posts dot the trail, and I recommend using the last marker at 3.5 miles as the turn-around. Beyond the marker the trail continues another one-fifth of a mile to Grizzly Peak Blvd. and the Lawrence Hall of Science, but this short distance is uphill and in my view an unnecessary exertion.

The return trip goes by very quickly because of the elevation loss and the entrancing views. Exercise caution on the steep downhill to the sundial, because the hard right turn at the base of the hill is difficult to negotiate if you're going fast.

Just north of the parking lot are the university's botanical gardens, which contain lush displays of flowers and plants. A stroll through these gardens is a pleasant way to relax after running. A little further still is the Lawrence Hall of Science, with its fascinating exhibits of mathematics, biology, mechanics, electronics, and astronomy. A noisier and less cerebral pastime might be a ride on Tilden Park's Steam Train, which is a few minutes drive further on Grizzly Peak Blvd. Among Tilden's other attractions are ten-

nis courts, swimming at Lake Anza (May thru September), a golf course, Environmental Education Center, and many picnic areas.

Directions to the Trail:

From Interstate 80 (Hwy 17) in Berkeley, take the University Ave. exit and go east through the city to Oxford St. Turn left at Oxford, then right on Hearst Ave. At Gayley Road turn right again, then left on Stadium Rim Way to Centennial Dr. Turn left on Centennial and park in the small dirt lot on the right just before you reach the U.C. Botanical Gardens.

Directions for the Run:

From the parking lot (**1**), take the dirt trail over Strawberry Creek. Continue to the sundial (**2**), then follow the trail left and sharply uphill. Continue on the trail to the 3.5-mile marker post (**3**), then turn around and retrace your steps to the parking lot.

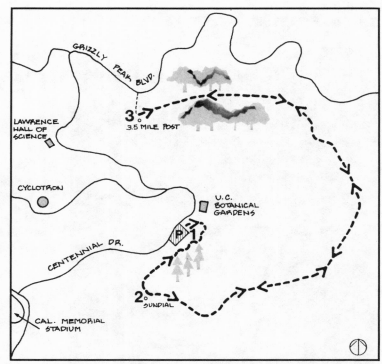

SANTA CLARA COUNTY

Coyote Creek/Hellyer Park

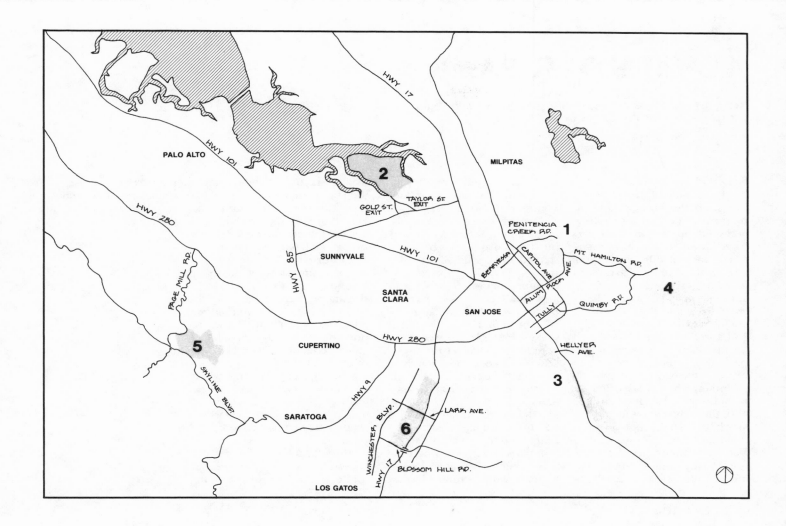

PALO ALTO

HWY 17

MILPITAS

HWY 101

2

GOLD ST. EXIT

TAYLOR ST. EXIT

HWY 280

PENITENCIA CREEK RD. 1

MT. HAMILTON RD.

HWY 85

SUNNYVALE

HWY 101

BERRYESSA

CAPITOL AVE.

ALUM ROCK AVE.

QUIMBY RD.

4

SANTA CLARA

TULLY

SAN JOSE

PAGE MILL RD.

HWY 280

CUPERTINO

HELLYER AVE.

5

SKYLINE BLVD.

3

HWY 9

WINCHESTER BLVD.

SARATOGA

LARK AVE.

6

HWY 17

BLOSSOM HILL RD.

LOS GATOS

ALUM ROCK PARK

Trail: *5.4 miles. Out-and-back with loop; some hills (North Rim); dirt; some pavement; 60% shade. Creek, woods, deer.*

General Description:

The foothills of the Diablo Range are the setting for this run on the Alum Rock Park's 700 acres. Founded in 1872, the park (then known only as the "reservation") was visited by people from all over the country who came to bathe in its famous mineral springs. During its heyday, between 1890 and 1932, visitors could ride to the park from San Jose for 25¢ on the Alum Rock Steam Railroad. Arriving at the park they would discover, in addition to the baths, an indoor swimming pool, a tea garden, a restaurant, and a dance pavilion.

In the twenty years following World War II, throngs of visitors from the booming Santa Clara Valley contributed to a deterioration of the facilities and the wildlife environment. Fortunately, the park has survived, now offering a more natural setting, picnicking, hiking, and horseback riding.

The first part of the trail follows Penitencia Creek eastward into the canyon and is cool, shaded and restful. Shortly after passing Eagle Rock Picnic Grounds you will cross the road and then recross it on a narrow bridge over which the steam railroad brought fashionable health-seekers in the 1800s. Here, on your left, you will see the large outcrop of rock once thought to contain the mineral alum, from which the park got its present name.

After nearly another mile, the trail takes you past the visitor center and the ornate water fountains and grottos where in former times the water's seven minerals would supposedly cure what ailed you. To your right is the Youth Science Institute, which is well worth a visit after the run. Here, for 50¢ (25¢ for children), you can mingle with hawks, crows, ravens, rabbits, owls, rattlesnakes, and assorted insects, all alive thanks to the efforts of the largely volunteer staff who care for the sick and injured animals.

On your way back, you will be taking the North Rim Trail, which puts you at a vantage point high above Penitencia Creek. Here the hillside is covered with grasses, sagebrush, and poison oak (which you can avoid if you stay on the trail), in contrast to the alder, maple, and sycamore trees which shaded the first part of your journey.

Alum Rock Park is favored by equestrians, so keep your eyes out for horses. If you wish to view the park from horseback yourself, stables are located on Alum Rock Road near the main entrance to the park.

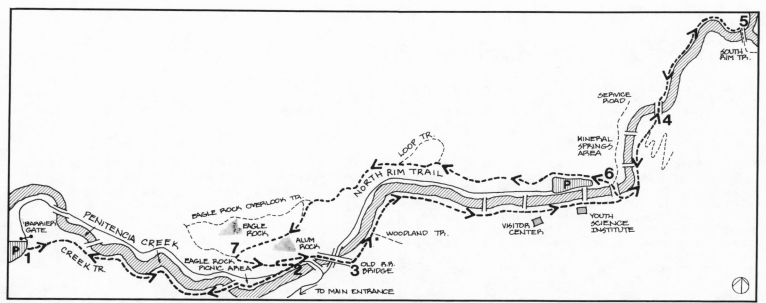

Directions to the Trail:

From Hwy 680 in San Jose, take Berryessa exit east to Capitol Ave. and turn right. At Penitencia Creek Road turn left and continue until the road ends at a barrier gate, then park.

Directions for the Run:

From the parking area (1), take Creek Trail east to Penitencia Creek and run beside it into the canyon. (If the trail is muddy, you can hop over the barrier gate and run on the paved road.) After passing Eagle Rock Picnic Grounds, cross the road (2) and pick up the trail on the other side, follow it and recross the road on Old Railroad Bridge (3). The marker for the Woodland Trail is the 1-mile point. Continue on Creek Trail (now paved) through the main area of the park, past the visitor center, Youth Science Institute and picnic areas and cross the creek again (4). Now you're on dirt, as the canyon narrows and the trees become more sparse. At 2.5 miles you come to another footbridge (5), after which the Creek Trail is closed. Here you *could* cross the bridge, climb the narrow, well-graded South Rim Switchback Trail, and follow it to Woodland Trail, which would take you back to Creek Trail and home. My preference, however, is to turn around and return on Creek Trail to the North Rim Trail (6), which begins roughly 500 feet before the Science Institute, near the large parking lot. Cross the bridge and make the fairly steep climb on a paved service road until it curves to the right, at which point you pick up the wide dirt trail and continue to climb. Continue past Loop Trail and Eagle Rock Overlook Trail, the 4-mile point. At the hairpin (7), leave North Rim Trail and branch downhill to the road (2). There you will once again pick up Creek Trail for a final jaunt through the trees to the finish.

Other Information:

Water and restrooms at visitor center; water at other locations. Visitor center.

Telephone number: Alum Rock Park, **(408)259-5477**.

ALVISO SLOUGH

Trail: *9 miles. Loop; flat; dirt/clay levees; exposed, sometimes windy. Bay views. Birds.*

General Description:

Alviso is a small town situated on the flatlands between Milpitas and Mountain View, at the southernmost tip of the San Francisco Bay. If you've heard of Alviso at all, it's probably because of the two huge sewage spills which wreaked havoc on the wildlife there, or the terrible flooding in recent years which did much the same to the human residents.

Don't let this notoriety deter you. A runner in search of a long, flat, solitary run will find it at Alviso Slough. This run provides views of both the East Bay and Peninsula hillsides, shimmering waters, and an opportunity to observe a diminished wildlife population recovering from disaster.

The run begins and ends at the marina, home to sea craft bearing a look of utility rather than the waxed and polished aura of recreational boats. Having left the marina behind, you follow a nine-mile hiking trail over a dirt and clay levee system upon which you encounter neither hill nor (usually) human. What you will encounter is a wide variety of birds, such as the avocet and the black-necked stilt, squawking their perfunctory warnings. An occasional heron or brown pelican will stand defiantly in your path, only to soar away at your approach.

A third of the way into the run, you pass the lush green Triangle Marsh, which presents a striking contrast to the water around it. I often wonder how many curious eyes are watching me from behind that tall emerald curtain.

As you continue out toward the bay, a silence envelops you. Only the sound of the water lapping against the levee accompanies the raucous birdcalls. The loneliness (or, more accurately, "aloneness") of the long-distance runner is never more strongly felt than here: no trees, no buildings, no traffic, only a flat expanse of water stretching away from the levee.

At the northernmost tip of the run you may well see a fishing boat or two going out in the choppy waters of the bay. As you come back toward the marina, the sights and sounds of civilization re-emerge. Moffett Field Naval Air Station off to the right, the urban sprawl of San Jose up ahead, and the clamor of traffic may serve to remind you that your car needs fixing or your house needs painting. But out there, for an hour, you had peace.

Following your run, you may find it interesting to wander around the marina. If you're hungry, there are a variety of Mexican and seafood restaurants nearby.

Directions to the Trail:

Take Hwy 237 which connects Hwys 101 and 17 in northern San Jose. Coming from Hwy 101 take Gold St. exit north to Elizabeth St. and turn left. Then turn right on Hope St. and follow it the short way to the marina parking lot.

From Hwy 17, take Taylor St. exit north to Hope St. and turn right to the marina parking lot.

Directions for the Run:

From the gate at the east end of the parking lot (**1**), take Alviso Slough Trail and follow it alongside the railroad tracks. At the trail marker (**2**) turn right, following the tracks for a short way, and then heading out beside the marshes. Turn right again at the next trail marker (**3**). A rocket-shaped hut (**4**) is the 5-mile point. Continue on the levee trail beside

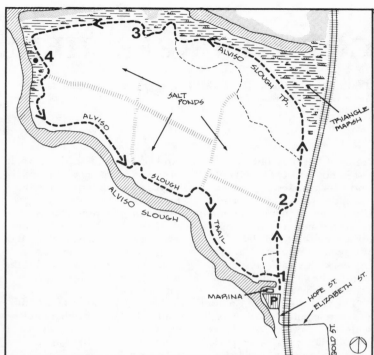

Alviso Slough. Pass the marina, turn right at the railroad tracks, and retrace your steps to the parking lot.

Other Information:

Water and restrooms at marina. Boat launch; picnic tables; nearby restaurants. Levees are closed periodically for repair. If it's windy or raining, don't go.

Telephone numbers: Marina information, (**408)358-13741**; Levee information (S.F. Bay National Wildlife Refuge), (**415)792-0222**.

COYOTE CREEK/HELLYER PARK

Trail: *12 miles. Out-and-back; gently rolling; paved; 60% shade. Creek, fields, orchards. Freeway and hillside views.*

General Description:

I'm not usually fond of out-and-back courses, but there are exceptions and Coyote Creek Trail is one of them. In addition to the advantage of being able to adjust the run to any length simply by turning around and heading back, this trail offers another bonus: the landscape looks different on the return trip.

The run is on a paved, almost flat bicycle path that borders the wide, fast-flowing Coyote Creek. It has a nice, rural feeling to it: once you leave the crowded picnic and play areas around Cottonwood Lake and pass under the freeway, pedestrian traffic is greatly reduced and the narrow path is sheltered by oak and maple trees. The meandering creek is to your right and farm-land lies to your left. The last half of the outward leg is bordered by fields, plum orchards, and some marshes, although you also get occasional glimpses of houses and the newly-constructed Bayshore Freeway. The turnabout point is at the dam for the percolation pond which is used for raising the water table for irrigation purposes.

The only disadvantage of this trail is the large number of bicyclists who use it, especially on weekends. But after all, it *is* a bike path.

After the run, Cottonwood Lake's one-half mile circumference can provide a pleasant warm-down walk. Often there are windsurf rentals available. The Olympic-sized velodrome is used for high-speed bicycle racing, and at certain hours the public can try their luck on the steeply banked track.

On the near side of Morgan Hill, a few miles south of Hellyer Park, Hwy 101 is lined with stands where you can buy a variety of fresh and inexpensive fruits and vegetables.

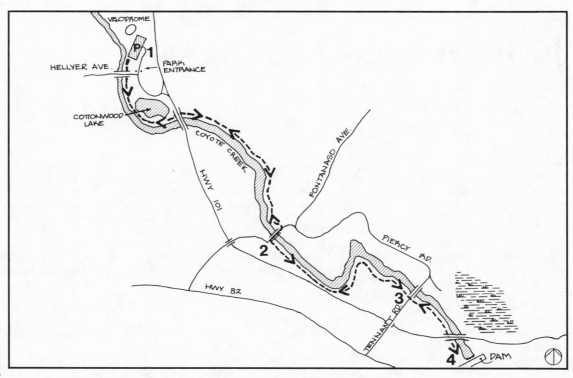

Direction to the Trail:

From Hwy 101 in San Jose, take Hellyer Ave. exit east to the park. Turn right into park and continue to the cycle velodrome parking lot.

Directions for the Run:

From the velodrome parking lot **(1)**, head south through the picnic grounds and under Hellyer Ave. on bike path. After passing under some shady cottonwood trees you reach Cottonwood Lake on your left, surrounded by grassy picnic and play areas. Proceed past the lake and under the freeway, and continue to Piercy Road **(2)**, the 3-mile point. Cross the bridge over the creek (watching out for traffic) and pick up the trail on the west bank. Cross Tennant Road **(3)**, the 5-mile point, and continue along the west bank. After passing some marshes on your left and going under a freeway overpass, you will come to a weir **(4)** at the base of a short steep rise, with a pond just beyond. This is the 6-mile point. Turn around and retrace the route back to the velodrome.

Other Information:

Water and restrooms at start/finish. Cycle velodrome; picnic areas; pond; sailboard rentals. Possible entrance fees.

Telephone number: Santa Clara Parks and Recreation Department, **(408)358-3741**.

JOSEPH D. GRANT PARK

Trail: *5.6 miles. Loop; some hills; dirt. Hillside and meadow views.*

General Description:

Originally part of a 15,714-acre land grant to José de Jesus Bernal in 1839, the 9,522 acres now known as Joseph D. Grant Park had many owners before its purchase by Santa Clara County in 1975. But the land itself remains largely unaltered, and today, as in Mexican times, cattle still graze on its grassy slopes and drink from its ponds and streams. Already well known to picnickers, hikers, and equestrians, many of the park's network of trails, especially those west of Mt. Hamilton Road, are well suited to a runner's needs.

This run is a rolling tour of a few of the park's less drastic hillsides, and while it does involve some climbing, the overall feel of the route is peaceful and relaxing. From the hillsides you can look over the entire valley. For me, it's reminiscent of a run over my uncle's farm in southern Ireland: not too much shade, but calming breezes, sweet-smelling grass, and a babbling brook.

The visitor center, at the beginning and end of the run, is full of interesting wildlife information. Many animals, some alive and others less fortunate, are displayed there. Remarkably, golden eagles still live in this park, despite its location just a few miles from San Jose. Even the bald eagle pays winter visits, and mountain lions have been spotted. A more likely sighting during the run would be a red-tailed hawk or a kestrel.

Stables are located near the main entrance, and many of the park's more arduous trails can be explored from the relative comfort of a rented horse.

By driving an extra eleven miles you can visit the James Lick Observatory, 4,200 feet above sea level, built in the late 1800's with funds provided by San Francisco millionaire James Lick. Both the 36-inch and 120-inch telescopes, used by the University of California, are shown to the public. A visitor center has technical literature on the subject if you care to learn more.

Roughly halfway between Alum Rock Ave. and Joseph D. Grant Park is the Rancho Grandview Restaurant, whose name is not an understatement: from the cocktail lounge or dining area, all of Santa Clara Valley is displayed. The original building, destroyed by fire in 1942, was a stopover point for the stagecoach on its way to the observatory.

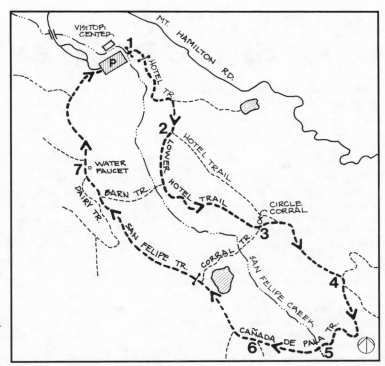

Directions to the Trail:

From Hwy 680 in San Jose, take Alum Rock Ave. exit east to Mt. Hamilton Road. Turn right and follow Hamilton seven and one-half miles southeast to the park. Follow the directions to the visitor center and park.

Alternative: From Hwy 101 in San Jose, take Tully Road exit east to Quimby Road. Turn right and follow Quimby to Mt. Hamilton Road. Turn right and continue to the park.

Directions for the Run:

Hop over the gate (1) near the visitor center parking lot and take Hotel Trail, quickly turn right at another gate and continue south to a fork in the trail (2). Go right on Lower Hotel Trail. Cross Barn Trail, the 1-mile point, and Corral Trail to the Circle Corral (3). Veer east through the Circle Corral and turn right back onto Hotel Trail again. Crossing a creek bed, the path leads to a two-stage climb. Turn right onto Cañada de Pala Trail (4), the 2.2-mile point, and take it down the hill to San Felipe Creek (5). (On the way to the creek is a well-posted rattlesnake area—be careful!) Cross the creek and climb. At 3.5 miles Cañada de Pala swings away, and you continue ahead on what is now San Felipe Trail (6). The worst hill is behind you now, and you run downward to a pond, the junction of Corral Trail, and another gate which represents the 4-mile mark. After passing Barn Trail, at the top of a short rise you will see on your right a water faucet attached to a horse trough (7); you can get a drink here. Soon the dirt trail yields to a newly surfaced road which you follow downhill, past picnic tables and restrooms to the finish.

Other Information:

Water and restrooms at start/finish. Visitor center; equestrian stables; picnic areas; wildlife. Possible entrance fees.

Telephone number: Park ranger, **(408)274-6121**.

MONTE BELLO OPEN SPACE PRESERVE

Trail: *5.8 miles. Loop; hilly; some pavement, mostly dirt; exposed, some shade. View of hill ranges.*

General Description:

Most Bay Area residents have picked up a rudimentary knowledge of earthquakes. For an opportunity to expand upon that knowledge and simultaneously have a good run, make the winding drive up Page Mill Road from Palo Alto to the Monte Bello Open Space Preserve. Here, and across the street at Los Trancos Open Space Preserve, you can see firsthand what earth movements can do and learn why they do it. These two areas, operated by the Midpeninsula Regional Open Space District, combine to form a 2,900-acre earthquake exhibit straddling the notorious San Andreas Fault.

Both preserves have trail systems for hikers and equestrians, but Monte Bello, being the larger of the two, is usually my choice for a run. Even on weekends the pathways are seldom busy, with most visitors keeping to the short self-guided nature trail adjacent to the parking lot. There are two main trails running the length of the preserve, one high on the ridge, the other in the canyon. This run will take you over sections of each trail, giving you a feel for the area. As is usually the case with such routes, some hill climbing is involved.

The climb up Black Mountain is rigorous, but is rewarded by a couple of breathtaking views of the South Bay. Standing at the summit (at 2,700 feet) you can see layer upon layer of the Santa Cruz Mountains.

On the steep run back down the wide trail you will be able to see the diversity of the flora in earthquake country. You will be running over the American Plate, whose soil encourages grass and chaparral rather than trees. This is in sharp contrast to the thicker vegetation seen in the canyon below, and also the Pacific Plate seen across to the west, whose soil supports forests of mixed evergreen and Douglas fir.

Coming along the Canyon Trail, you will be following the San Andreas Fault, which you may find interesting if not comforting. On the right you will see a sag pond, created when the two plates were forced apart and the subsequent void filled with water and silt, producing abundant plant life.

Docent-led walks in both Monte Bello and Los Trancos are available, but if you wish to explore on your own, you'll find excellent brochures at both locations which will help explain the curious land that surrounds you.

The delightful town of Saratoga is only a fifteen-minute drive away. Its numerous restaurants and bars are a good reason to make the journey. Three more good reasons are the Saratoga Historical Society, the Japanese Gardens, and the Paul Masson Vineyards. On your way there, look out for the Congress Springs Winery a few miles east of Hwy 35 on Hwy 9. It is open for tasting on Friday, Saturday, and Sunday.

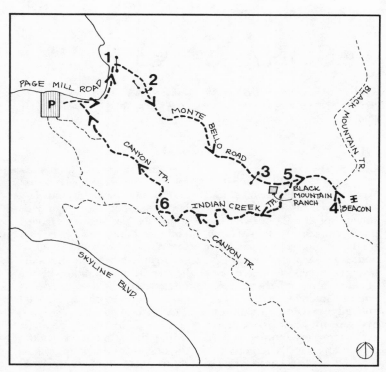

Directions to the Trail:

From Hwy 280 in Palo Alto, take Page Mill Road exit west seven and one-half miles to the parking area on the left of the road.

From Saratoga, take Hwy 9 north to Skyline Blvd. (Hwy 35). Take Hwy 35 north. Turn right on Page Mill Road and continue one and one-half miles to the parking lot.

Directions for the Run:

From the parking lot run east on Page Mill Road to the gate (1) at the start of Monte Bello Road (now closed to traffic) and turn right. Climb past the large gateway on the right, the 1-mile mark (2), where the pavement is replaced by broken asphalt and dirt. Veer left, staying on the main trail, pass through a gate you must open and close (3), the 2.5-mile mark, and climb the remaining one-fifth of a mile to the top of the hill. Turn around at the aircraft beacon (4). Retrace your steps back down to Indian Creek Trail (5), the 3-mile mark, and take it to the left. A hard left U-turn is followed by a hard right, marking 4 miles. Come down to the junction with Canyon Trail (6), turn right, and follow Canyon Trail back to Page Mill Road. Turn left and return to the parking lot.

Other Information:

No water. Portable toilets are at the start and finish. Docent-led walks; nature trail.

Telephone number: Midpeninsula Regional Open Space District, **(415)965-4717.**

VASONA LAKE PARK

Trail: *5.5 miles. Out and back with a small loop; flat; paved, some dirt. Reservoir, creek. Residential, industrial, and distant hillside views.*

General Description:

The problem of meeting the Bay Area's soaring demand for water is well known, as are the various solutions: pipelines from the Sierra, construction of large reservoirs, percolation ponds, etc. Some of these measures have brought unexpected recreational benefits along with them, as is demonstrated by Vasona Lake, created by a dam for the purpose of raising the water level to permit gravity flow to a number of percolation ponds. These ponds, in turn, allow the water to seep into the groundwater basins which service Santa Clara Valley homes, industry, and farms.

Vasona Lake Park has become one of the hottest attractions in Santa Clara County—some would say too hot, especially on summer weekends when it is filled to capacity. But fear not. While crowds come for the picnic grounds, large lawns, and sailboating, runners soon leave the busy park behind. Following the tree-lined banks of fast-flowing Los Gatos Creek, your route borders homes and light industrial buildings before it reaches the sparsely shaded expanse of the percolation ponds. The farthest pond, whose banks you will circle, is also a popular fishing hole. Coming back along the far side of the ponds, the slopes of Mt. Hamilton are visible to the east.

After your run, you might want to stroll over the footbridge and under the trees to the Vasona Sailing Center and rent a boat. Users of Vasona Lake Park appear to be fair weather types, and, though it is true that resources are stretched on summer weekends, midweek and off-season usage is light. These are the best times to enjoy the natural beauty of the lake and the admirable landscaping surrounding it.

Another of the park's attractions (actually originating in the adjacent Oak Meadow Park) is the Billy Jones Wildcat Railroad, a narrow gauge system which begins running around Easter time.

For some zany fun, you might try a tour of the Winchester Mystery House, a few miles from the park on Winchester Blvd. Designed to confuse the evil spirits who had the misfortune to pick on Sarah Winchester, heiress to the Winchester Arms fortune, the 160 rooms of this mansion have managed to befuddle all who enter—even the servants required maps to aid in the negotiation of the 2,000 doors, secret passageways, and some 40 stairways.

Directions to the Trail:

From Hwy 17 in Los Gatos, take Lark Ave. exit west to Winchester Blvd. and turn left. Continue to Blossom Hill Road and turn left. The park entrance is on your left, just after Oak Meadow Park. Turn into Vasona Lake Park and follow Garden Hill Dr. to the right of the lake. Park between the restrooms and the fishing pier.

Directions for the Run:

From the fishing pier on the eastern side of the lake, take the bike path through the eucalyptus trees and past a couple of picnic areas to the dam (1). Continuing on the bike path along the right side of the creek, you will come to busy Lark Ave. (2), the 1-mile mark. By crossing the creek on the south side of the road, another path will take you safely under the traffic without interrupting your run. You will now be on the left side of the creek, running beside Charter Oaks Dr., where there are several alterna-

tive parking areas in case the Vasona Lake Park area is too full. Industrial buildings will show themselves briefly, and beside a footbridge crossing the creek (3), at 2.1 miles, you emerge into the open space of the Camden Percolation System. The trail threads between the collection ponds and the creek until, at the parking lot in Los Gatos Park (4), you leave the trail to turn left on the road, following the outside of the last pond. Keep to the edge of the pond and turn left again on the dirt path on the western shore. Follow the trail back to the bike path and the footbridge, turn right, and retrace your outward journey.

Other Information:

Water fountains and restrooms in the park. Boat rentals and lessons; picnic areas; snack bars; miniature railroad; fishing. Possible entrance fees.

Telephone number: Park office, **(408)358-3741**.

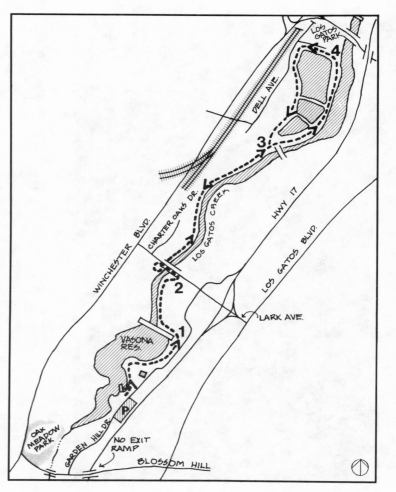

Sawyer Camp Historic Trail

SAN MATEO COUNTY

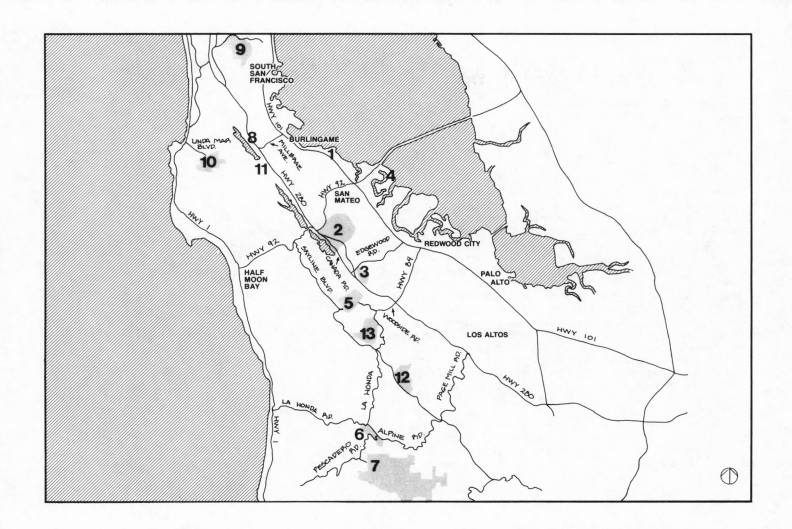

COYOTE POINT COUNTY PARK

Trail: *4.4 miles. Loop with out-and-back section; gently rolling; mostly paved; 50% shade. Bay views. Eucalyptus groves.*

General Description:

Located just south of San Francisco Airport and bordering the bay, Coyote Point Park is a good place to visit on those days when you want to do something but you're not sure what. Its 670 acres are full of recreational diversions, and this pleasant, non-taxing run is a good way to acquaint yourself with the park's amenities.

You can expect, however, to find large numbers of visitors here, especially on weekends.

For the most part you'll stay on the paved perimeter footpath as it winds around the park in a gently rolling motion which should be comfortable for runners at all levels of proficiency—especially since cool breezes can be expected from the bay.

Leaving the beach and heading uphill into a eucalyptus grove, you pass the Castaway Restaurant which features Polynesian cuisine and overlooks the water. Cresting the hill, you cruise around the north end of the park beside a museum which houses many native animals and has exhibits describing the area's ecology. Soon you'll see the family picnic area to the right and the modern marina, bristling with sailboats, to the left.

The flat, exposed bicycle path leading away from the marina offers a greater degree of solitude. The run along the water's edge is pleasant, despite the proximity of power lines and pylons that detract from the setting.

Back on the perimeter path, the fairways of the City of San Mateo Golf Course are to your left, and soon the rifle range, which is open to the public, appears nestled in the trees to your right.

Runners with young children might appreciate the large adventure playground, the next attraction you pass. Later, the kids can work off their surplus steam here while you try to regain some of yours.

The last leg of this jaunt takes you along the promenade beside the beach. A brisk swim in the bay (if you're daring) followed by a little sun worship is as good a way as I can think of to end a run. Lying on the beach, you can see aircraft from around the world making their final approaches to San Francisco Airport.

Map labels:

SAN FRANCISCO BAY

MARINA

CASTAWAY RESTAURANT

MUSEUM

ANIMAL CENTER

PARK HDQTRS.

START/FINISH

P

RIFLE RANGE

P

P

P

6

P

PLAYGROUND

5

PARK ENTRANCE

COYOTE POINT DR.

CITY OF SAN MATEO GOLF COURSE

4

YACHT CLUB

P

AIRPORT BLVD.

COYOTE POINT DR.

HWY 101 BAYSHORE FWY

2

1

7

3

E. THIRD AVE.

Directions to the Run:

Heading south on Hwy 101 in Burlingame, take the Poplar Ave. exit and follow signs to the park. Heading north on Hwy 101 in Burlingame take the Dore exit, turn left onto Bayshore and follow signs to the park.

After entering the park, follow the signs to the Castaway Restaurant and park at the beach near the restrooms.

Directions for the Run:

From the beach parking area, take the footpath past the Castaway Restaurant into the eucalyptus grove. At the vista point (1) keep left and curve past the museum around the north end of a parking area to the marina. Follow the marina to its southern most tip (2), cross the road to the bike path, and follow it beside the power lines to East 3rd Ave. (3), the 1.8-mile mark. (The run can be extended by continuing on the bike path beyond East 3rd Ave.) Turn around and retrace your steps to the southern tip of the marina, cross the road into the eucalyptus grove, turn left onto the bike path (4), the 3-mile mark, and follow the path to the park entrance gate (5). Turn right onto the jogging path and continue to the beach (6). Turn right and continue to the finish.

Other Information:

Restrooms and water fountains at start/finish and on route. Beach; marina; museum; rifle range; playgrounds; golf course. Two dollar park entrance fee.

Telephone number: Park Information, (415)573-2592.

CRYSTAL SPRINGS LOOP

Trail: *6.7 miles. Loop; hills; dirt, 30% paved; mostly exposed. Freeway and residential views. Reservoir, wooded watershed lands.*

General Description:

This run through some of San Francisco's watershed lands in San Mateo County is actually a combination of four trails, each with differing characteristics. The six and one-half mile loop leads you beside a lake, past a temple, over grassy hills, down a wooded canyon, past expensive homes, and over, under, and alongside a freeway. Despite the blatant clash of wilderness and civilization— or perhaps because of it—the Crystal Springs Loop is a good run; its constantly changing scenery and terrain simultaneously prevent boredom and challenge the runner.

The first leg takes you down a narrow dirt trail, bobbing up and down through small wooded copses beside the Crystal Springs Lake. The lake is a stopover point for water birds in the Pacific Flyway; keep your eyes open in winter for flocks of Canadian geese. Throughout the year deer can be seen browsing and drinking along the shores.

After three miles you come to the Pulgas Water Temple. The temple's tall pillars and shallow pool, built to commemorate the completion of the O'Shaughnessy Dam at Hetch Hetchy and the subsequent flow of Sierra Nevada waters into Crystal Springs Lake, are surrounded by manicured lawns and tall oak trees.

Making a U-turn at the temple, you follow Canada Road to the Sheep Camp Trail which heads inland, uphill through small, grassy meadows, and past scattered oak trees. A glance over your shoulder reveals a lovely view of the lake, with the thickly wooded hillsides rising above it.

The first harsh contrast comes as you pass under the Junipero Serra Freeway (Hwy 280) and climb above it on a paved trail toward hilltop homes. Once among the houses the character of the run changes from wilderness to suburban. You can enjoy a brief period of seclusion in a grove of tall eucalyptus trees as you head down the dirt-surfaced Waterdog Trail. The return to civilization is heralded by a grand view of attractive Belmont homes.

Running past new homes and condominiums you arrive at a bike path which skirts a chaparral-coated ridge alongside Hwy 92. This trail climbs to a concrete span above Hwy 280, where you can pause to look at the scurrying traffic far below before dropping back down the trail, with the watershed lands spread before you, to the starting point.

A visit to the Pulgas Water Temple is a splendid way to relax after the run, but it requires parking your car on the road about one-half mile from the entrance and hoofing it the rest of the way. If you make the effort on a hot day, the words from the book of Isaiah inscribed upon the temple's pediment take on a special significance: "I give waters in the wilderness and rivers in the desert to give drink to my people."

Directions to the Trail:

From Hwy 280 near San Mateo take Hwy 92 exit west toward Half Moon Bay. Turn onto Canada Road and park alongside the road.

Directions for the Run:

From the parking area on Canada Road, pick up Crystal Springs Trail (1) and follow it south to the Pulgas Water Temple (2). (In the summertime, the trail may be overgrown with tall thistles. If so, use the bicycle lane alongside Canada Road.) Make a U-turn and run beside the highway (there's a bike lane) north to Sheep Camp Trail (3), and take it inland to Hwy 280. Pass under the freeway and pick up the trail again at the gate (4). Continue uphill to St. James Road (5), cross it, and follow Waterdog Trail down to Hallmark Dr. (6) and turn left. At Ralston Ave. (7) turn left again and follow the bike path to the "Park and Ride" parking area (8). Make another left, paralleling Hwy 92 on the paved bike path, over the freeway to Canada Road and back to the finish.

Other Information:

Canada Road is closed to automotive traffic on the first and third Sundays of the month from April to October, to accommodate cyclists who tour and race here. The parking area is not affected.

Telephone number: San Mateo County Parks and Recreation Dept., (415)363-4020.

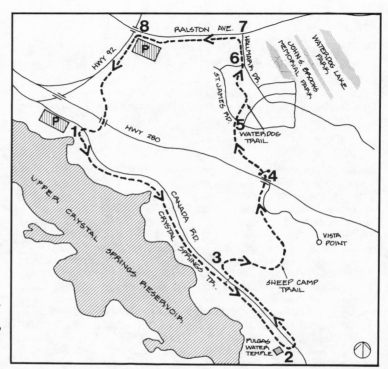

EDGEWOOD COUNTY PARK

Trail: *3.5 miles. Loop; graded hills; dirt; mostly shaded. Views of surrounding hills, watershed lands, freeway and South Bay. Wildflowers.*

General Description:

Edgewood Park's 477 acres cannot boast of adventure playgrounds, landscaped picnic areas, or other public facilities that can be found in many of the larger, more established parks in San Mateo County. It does, however, provide a network of hiking and equestrian trails, most shaded by oak trees or bordered by grassy meadows which are covered with wildflowers in the spring. Once a stomping ground for off-road vehicles and dirt bikes, this newly reopened park is healing its wounds very successfully. Runners, hikers, and horseback riders are now able to enjoy the rare flowers and wildlife without noisy interruptions. Runners must keep an eye out for both horses and poison oak, though. A collision

with either on the narrow trail can be most unpleasant.

The run I have suggested here is short, well marked, and only moderately strenuous. It takes you through a wooded canyon where you'll have an occasional glimpse of the surrounding hillsides and scattered homes, across the side of a grassy ridge, and back down oak-shaded switchbacks. If you wish a slightly more difficult run, take the Ridgeview Scenic Overlook Trail to the summit of the hill which dominates the area. From the top are splendid views of Skyline Ridge and the San Francisco watershed to the west, Redwood City and the bay to the east.

Despite the hilly configuration of the park, its trails are well graded, not overly arduous and

usually deserted. These features, along with the relatively short distances involved, make these trails ideal for putting in a little cross-country jaunt on 'light' training days.

A blanket, a picnic basket, and bottle of wine might be worthwhile additions to your running gear here. Observant picnickers are often rewarded with sights and sounds of the area's wildlife going about its business amongst the trees or on the surrounding slopes.

Directions to the Trail:

From Hwy 280 west of Redwood City, take Edgewood Road east to the parking area just past Crestview Dr.

Directions for the Run:

Start at the Old Stagecoach Road entrance on Edgewood Road, opposite the beginning of Crestview Dr. From the parking area, cross the bridge (1) and go straight. Follow the trail around a 'U' bend in front of the steep service road (2), continue to the fork (3), and go right. At the 'T' junction (4), go left onto Sylvan Loop Trail to the fork with the trail to Sylvan Way (5) and go right. Continue a few yards past the junction with Serpentine Trail (6), and go right. At the next junction (7) go hard right, continue to the crossroads (8), and go diagonally left on the narrow trail. At the fork with Edgewood Trail (9) go right on Ridgeview Loop to the junction with Ridgeview Scenic Overlook Trail (10). Continue on Ridgeview Loop to Serpentine Trail (11) and follow Serpentine Trail past Sylvan Loop Trail (12), crossing over the service road, and at Edgewood Trail (13) veer right and take it to finish at the bridge.

Other Information:

Although there are three entrances to the park, none is well marked as yet. By far the easiest to find is the Old Stagecoach Road entrance on Edgewood Road. Parking is adequate here.

Telephone numbers: Edgewood County Park, (415)851-7570; San Mateo County Parks and Recreation Dept., (415)363-4020.

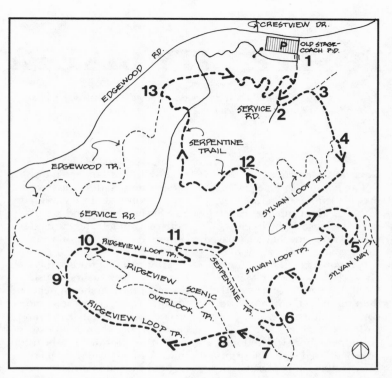

FOSTER CITY BIKE PATH

Trail: *6.5 miles. Out-and-back; flat; paved; exposed, can be windy. Views of Bay Area, aircraft, San Mateo Bridge, and fishing pier.*

General Description:

The Foster City bike path can provide runners of all abilities with a pleasant run over easy terrain. It is close to the freeway, with easy parking, has a flat, paved surface, and offers a view of the bay. If you have to commute on Hwy 92 across the San Mateo Bridge or past 92 on Hwy 101, then this path might appeal to you as an alternative to facing rush hour traffic.

Your run here will undoubtedly be shared with other runners, walkers, bicyclists, but the path can accommodate everyone and has a friendly air. A lot of women runners use this trail, probably because the completely exposed path and the nearness of homes and stores make the area reassuringly safe.

As you head south from the shadow of the San Mateo Bridge, the city noise fades. You have quite a contrast of views, with the San Francisco Bay and East Bay Hills on your left and the modern homes of Foster City on your right.

After running for two miles, you leave the road and housing tracts for the marshes of Belmont Slough. Apart from the sound of aircraft approaching San Francisco Airport, there is little to detract from the quiet for the next mile. A small picnic area on the right of the path marks the turn-around. The bike path continues past some new condominiums, but I've never travelled it, preferring to go for longer runs in less urban surroundings.

On the return trip you can see—fog, haze or smog permitting—San Francisco, the Bay Bridge, and Oakland, and the impressive San Mateo Bridge stretching forever, it seems, toward Hayward. No matter what the weather, you can usually see a few people trying their luck at fishing from the waterside benches beside the trail.

Directions to the Trail:

From Hwy 92 in Foster City, take Foster City Blvd. south to East Hillsdale Blvd. and turn left. Continue to the San Mateo County Fishing Pier parking lot.

Directions for the Run:

From the fishing pier (1), follow the bike path south. The 1-mile mark is a sign on your left informing dog owners to leash their dogs because they're in a sensitive wildlife area. The intersection with Foster City Blvd. is the 2-mile mark. Turn around at the small picnic area (2), which marks 3.25 miles, and return. The end of the marshy area roughly makes the 4-mile point; the playing fields on the left are an even 5 miles.

Other Information:

At the 1-mile mark, if you look in an 11 o'clock direction across the bay, you'll see Coyote Hills Regional Park just to the north of the Dumbarton Bridge. A suggested Coyote Hills run can be found elsewhere in this book (see pages 58-59).

Telephone number: San Mateo County Fishing Pier Information, **(415)573-2593**.

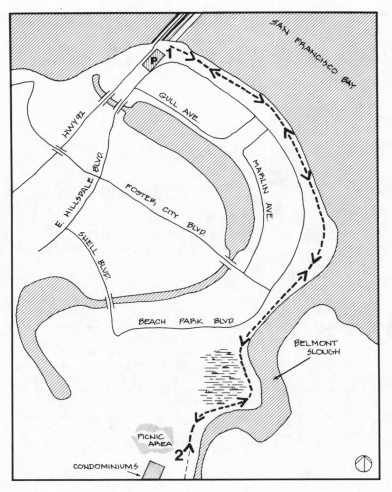

HUDDART PARK

Trail: *5 miles. Loop; rolling; dirt; mostly shaded. Hill and canyon views. Streams; second-growth redwood forest.*

General Description:

The town of Woodside borders one of San Mateo's finest parks. Driving past the expansive ranches and beautiful, secluded homes of this area is sure to put you in the mood to run the quiet, shaded trails of Huddart Park.

Once part of John Coppinger's 12,550-acre ranch, a grant from the Mexican Governor of California in 1840, the 1,000 acres which make up the park have seen, suffered, and survived much. In the 1850s and '60s, most of the redwoods that grew on these hillsides were logged and removed to one of the many nearby sawmills. But second-growth redwoods, oak, laurel, madrone, and Douglas fir have all but succeeded in concealing the scars inflicted a hundred years ago.

The trail described here is one of numerous trails in this area, several of which are part of San Mateo County's "Jogging and Exercise" system, marked with mileage markers. The one I've chosen will take you along a creek from the park's oak-forested lower elevations up through a corner of the chaparral-covered slopes found at higher altitudes. Lofty redwoods shade most of the route. The trail is wide and well maintained, although it can get muddy in wet weather.

The run begins on Richard's Road Trail, once the route taken by wagons carrying lumber to the Redwood City embarcadero where it was barged to an eagerly awaiting San Francisco. The damp smell of rich undergrowth permeates the air as you run beneath a canopy of trees, following a stream. After you cross the stream at one mile, the next couple of miles are up and down, with two series of graded switchbacks that will test your legs. After crossing McGarvey Gulch Creek, the rest is pleasantly downhill, as you descend into Werder Flat, go around the picnic grounds, and head back to Richard's Road Trail.

Picnic grounds are abundant at Huddart Park, and the Meadow Picnic Area has barbecue pits, volleyball areas, and horseshoe pitching.

Food and drink can be found in Woodside. If you feel like driving, you can take Skyline north to Hwy 92 and head over to Half Moon Bay and the ocean.

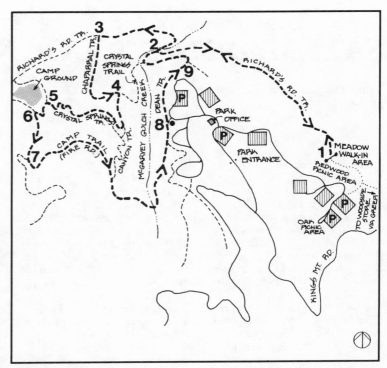

Directions to the Trail:

From Hwy 280 in Woodside, take Woodside Road west and continue to King's Mountain Road. Turn right and follow King's Mountain Road past the Woodside Store to the park access road. Turn right and continue to the entrance. Keep right and park near the Oak or Redwood picnic areas. (If these areas are closed, you may have to park at the entrance and walk to the start of the run.)

Directions for the Run:

From the Meadow Walk-In Area, walk northwest to the beginning of the designated jogging trail at the gate (1). Follow Richard's Road Trail to the hairpin bend crossing the creek (2). Cross and climb, passing the 1-mile marker, to narrow Chaparral Trail (3), and turn left onto it. Go downhill to Crystal Springs Trail (4), and take it to the right. Go uphill, past Canyon Trail and the 2-mile marker, turn left at the fork marked 'Campground' (5), and left again at the next

fork (6) toward 'Skyline'. Turn left onto the wide fire road, which is Camp Trail (7). Cross McGarvey Gulch Creek, and turn left onto Dean Trail at the water tower (8). Follow Dean Trail around the Werder Flat Picnic Area to the hard U-turn (9) after the 4-mile marker. Take the U-turn and follow the trail down to the creek and the junction with Richard's Road Trail (2). Retrace your steps to the finish at the gate.

For a longer run don't drive into the park, but begin your workout at the historic Woodside Store, built in 1853. Run the short way up King's Mountain Road and turn right onto Greer Road. Some very pleasant running under arched trees and past expensive homes will bring you to the park boundary, the path to Meadow Walk-In Area, and the route described above. This will add approximately two miles to the run.

Other Information:

Water and toilets are at the start/finish and on route. Picnic areas; barbecue pits; nature trail; equestrian use; playgrounds. Possible parking fee.

Telephone numbers: Park ranger, **(415)851-0326**; San Mateo County Parks and Recreation Dept., **(415)363-4020**.

SAM McDONALD COUNTY PARK

Trail: *4 miles. Loop; hilly; dirt; shaded. Views of hillsides, ocean. Redwood groves, pastures.*

General Description:

Sam McDonald Park is a good location for a short or medium run prior to a day of exploring, picnicking, or beachcombing. Named for its one-time owner who willed this land to the county, the park is steep and rugged. But the trails that wind up and down through its 870 acres are mostly shaded and soft underfoot.

This run begins on Forest Loop Trail, a marked trail which does much to showcase the park. Heading north, the trail switchbacks wind uphill through the dense redwoods, allowing brief glimpses of the distant hillsides. After leaving Forest Loop Trail, climbing up the steep Ridge Trail, and crossing Pescadero Road, hillsides unfold one after the other toward the ocean, which is visible when the sky is clear. Then

it's downhill through more redwoods and out upon grassy hills which resemble freshly fluffed pillows casually thrown about. Leaving the grassy knolls behind, near the Jack Brook Horse Camp, turn left and continue downhill in shade to once again cross Pescadero Road. The final yards of the run are on a narrow footpath through more magnificent trees.

If you haven't tired of redwoods by this time, you can take a drive one mile east on Alpine Road to Heritage Grove. Here you will find thirty-seven acres of gloriously unspoiled first-growth redwoods. Also nearby are Memorial County Park, the towns of Loma Mar and Pescadero, and the Pacific Ocean. (See Pescadero Creek Trail, pages 110-111, for more information.)

Directions to the Trail:

From Skyline Blvd. (Hwy 35) in Sky Londa, take La Honda Road (Hwy 84) south to Pescadero Road, turn left and continue to the park. The entrance is on the right after passing Alpine Road.

If coming from the south, take Alpine Road south from Skyline, continue to Pescadero Road, and turn left. The park entrance will be on your right.

Directions for the Run:

From the parking area, go north on Forest Loop Trail on the switchbacks. When you come to the fork with the wide Ridge Trail (1), go left and uphill to Pescadero Road (2). Cross Pescadero and continue climbing on Ridge Trail, with wooded hillsides and the ocean to your right. Continue on Ridge Trail, going downhill to the grasslands. At the junction with Towne Trail (3) turn left, going downhill across Pescadero Road (4) to park headquarters.

Other Information:

Water and toilets at start/finish and at the Jack Brook Horse Camp on Towne Trail.

Telephone numbers: Sam McDonald Park Headquarters, **(415)747-0403**; San Mateo County Parks and Recreation Dept, **(415)363-4020**.

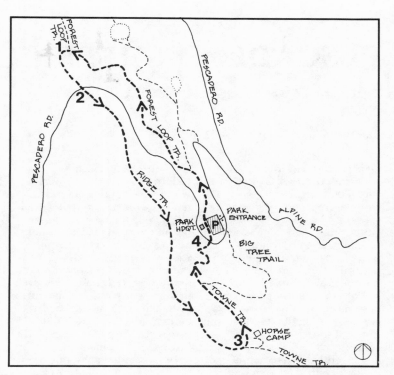

PESCADERO CREEK COUNTY PARK

Trail: *12 miles. Out-and-back; gently rolling; dirt; mostly shaded. Redwoods.*

General Description:

Pescadero Creek County Park, with 6,000 acres of redwoods and Douglas firs, is one of the peninsula's best kept secrets, allowing runners to put in some serious (or not so serious) training in peace and quiet, surrounded by natural beauty and watched only by inquisitive animals.

The run I've chosen is a simple out-and-back course covering a twelve-mile, moderately hilly trail through second-growth redwoods.

This entire area has a history of heavy logging, and a few unpleasant reminders are still visible from the trail. Not too far from the halfway mark, for instance, a steel cable remains wrapped around a redwood, rusted but unyielding. Despite past excesses, second-growth trees are plentiful.

There are no facilities at Pescadero Creek Park, but Memorial County Park, just a quarter of a mile west on Pescadero Road, has all you need: restrooms, water fountains, shady picnic grounds, and a swimming hole complete with its own tiny beach. All of these amenities are within a forest of towering redwoods, some even first-growth giants. If you want to remain overnight, this park, the oldest in the San Mateo area, offers year-round camping facilities on a first-come basis.

In Loma Mar, a few miles west, is a vegetarian restaurant called the Blue-Eyed Goose. A little further still, in the town of Pescadero, is Duarte's Tavern, renowned for its home cooking. The ocean with its spacious beaches is only a fifteen-minute drive from the start of the run.

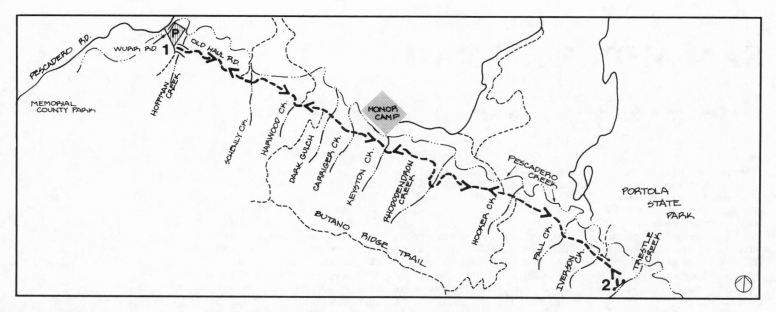

Directions to the Trail:

From Skyline Blvd. (Hwy 35) in Sky Londa, take La Honda Road (Hwy 84) south and go left at Pescadero Road. Follow it past Alpine Road to Wurr Road (one-quarter mile before reaching Memorial County Park), turn left, cross the creek, and park.

If coming from the south on Skyline, go south on Alpine Road (a continuation of Page Mill Road) to Pescadero Road. Turn left to Wurr Road, cross the creek and park.

Directions for the Run:

From the parking lot on Wurr Road, cross the bridge (1) onto Old Haul Road. Follow it east to Trestle Creek barrier gate (2) just past the entrance to neighboring Portola State Park, and return.

Other Information:

At nearby Memorial County Park are restrooms and water fountains, camping sites, picnic tables, and a swimming area.

Telephone number: San Mateo County Parks and Recreation Dept., **(415)456-1286.**

SAN ANDREAS TRAIL

Trail: *4 miles. Out-and-back; gently rolling; part paved, part dirt; 30% shade. Views of lake and watershed land.*

General Description:

Although the out-and-back San Andreas Trail closely parallels Skyline Blvd. and the 280 freeway, westward views of San Andreas Lake with its backdrop of densely forested hillsides make this a very pleasant Peninsula run. Frequent breezes and a gently rolling terrain are added attractions.

From the northern end of the trail, Sweeny Ridge lies to the west, beyond the lake. This is where Gaspar de Portolá first laid eyes on the San Francisco Bay. A future trail is planned to pass by Portola's discovery site, connecting the San Andreas Trail to San Pedro Park on the coastal side of the ridge.

The lake itself fills the valley where Indians once made their homes. The Spanish grazed their cattle here, but did not live on the land—supposedly because the livestock attracted large numbers of grizzly bears. In the mid-1800s white settlers were still defending their animals from bears and mountain lions, and even today a few wildcats are thought to roam the untouched woodlands west of the lake.

At Larkspur Dr. the paved bike path gives way to a tree-lined, dirt equestrian trail, which closely follows the freeway. Built by Caltrans to replace the riding and hiking trail which was lost during the construction of Hwy 280, this short section is shielded from too much freeway noise, and a bed of pine needles makes it soft underfoot.

The turnaround point is at Hillcrest Blvd. where the Sawyer Camp Trail begins (see pages 118-119).

There are no amenities on the San Andreas Trail. It is simply a short, easy-to-follow path in attractive surroundings. Even its closeness to the freeway can be an advantage to harried commuters in search of a running 'fix' on their way home—a fact that has not escaped the many runners who use this trail.

Directions to the Trail:

Going north on Hwy 280 in Millbrae, take Skyline Blvd. exit, and go north on Skyline to the parking area.

Going south on 280 in San Bruno, take Sneath Lane exit. Stay on Frontage Road to San Bruno Ave., turn right to Skyline, and go left about one-quarter mile to the parking area.

Note: if you plan to start at the south end of the trail, see directions for Sawyer Camp Trail.

Directions for the Run:

From parking area (1) go south on the bike path to Larkspur Dr. (2). Pick up the narrow dirt trail beside the freeway and follow it to Hillcrest Blvd. (3) and return.

Other Information:

Water at gas station at Hillcrest and Skyline.

If you add the Sawyer Camp Trail to your run, you will have an eight-mile one-way run or a sixteen-mile round-trip run.

Telephone number: San Mateo County Parks and Recreation Dept., **(415)363-4020.**

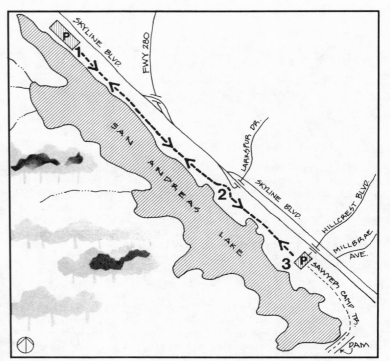

SAN BRUNO MOUNTAIN

Trail: *4 miles. Out-and-back; hilly; dirt; exposed, can be windy or foggy; marked every half mile. Views of ocean, bay, Bay Area cities, airport. Wildflowers.*

General Description:

No finer view can be found on the peninsula than from the top of San Bruno Mountain. Luckily for runners, a jogging trail exists, courtesy of the San Mateo County Parks and Recreation Dept., that allows you to enjoy that view while running four miles.

A wide dirt trail from the mountain's 1,314-foot summit takes you on a roller coaster ride along Ridge Trail to East Peak, two miles away. The run can be taxing in places, but 360-degree vistas and an uncrowded trail more than compensate for the exertion. Stretched out before you are distant mountains, the Pacific Ocean, San Francisco's magnificent skyline, the bay itself, and the other cities that line the shores of the bay. If the fog has shrouded the mountain, a totally

different experience awaits you: a run in swirling mists on the exposed ridge surrounded by scrub and grassy slopes is eerie, yet serenely beautiful. It can, on occasion, get quite breezy up here, so you might want to bring a jacket just in case.

San Bruno Mountain has changed little since the days of the Spanish when cattle roamed its slopes—though over the years it has narrowly escaped development plans, including one to remove the mountaintop for use as land fill. Prior to its becoming a park in 1978, the land was much abused by four-wheel drive vehicles and motorcycles. Nowadays, great pains are being taken to repair the damage. Few trees are found on the mountain, but numerous varieties of grasses and wildflowers seem to find the place

to their liking, as do four very rare butterflies, the San Francisco Silverspot, the Mission Blue, the San Bruno Elfin, and the Bay Checkerspot.

Several other trails have been

cleared and are marked near the entrance to the park. In the spring, April Brook Trail is a good bet because of the splendid array of wildflowers.

Directions to the Trail:

Going south on Hwy 280 in Daly City, take Eastmoor exit and go left on Sullivan Ave. beside the freeway. Go left on San Pedro Road and continue as it becomes Market, then Guadalupe Canyon Pkwy to the park entrance. Follow the entrance road (Radio Road) to its end and park.

Going north on Hwy 280, take Mission exit and turn left onto Junipero Serra Blvd. and then right onto San Pedro Road. Cross Mission onto Market and continue to the park entrance.

Directions for the Run:

From the gate (1) at the east end of the parking area, head east to East Peak (2), the 2-mile point, and return.

Other Information:

Portable toilet at park entrance. Possible parking fee.

Telephone number: San Mateo County Parks and Recreation Dept., **(415)363-4020**.

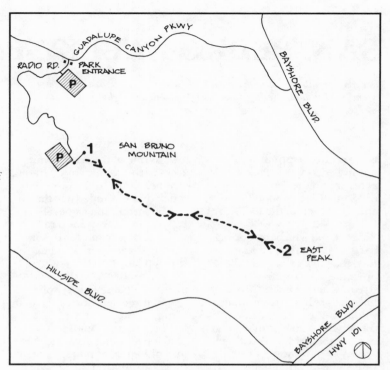

SAN PEDRO VALLEY PARK

Trail: *3.5 miles. Loop with an out-and-back; mostly flat; dirt, some pavement; 40% shade. Creeks, wooded canyons, and pastureland; wildlife.*

General Description:

San Pedro Valley Park's 1,150 acres are on the western edge of the Santa Cruz mountain range, almost hidden in the foothills of Pacifica. Sitting below Sweeney Ridge, from which the Portolá party first saw the San Francisco Bay, the park's wooded valleys, open meadows, year-round streams, and chaparral-covered hillsides are home to an abundant wildlife. A few short running trails, which can be run separately or in sequence for added distance, allow you to witness some of the valley's beauty first-hand, and, with the exception of busy weekends, in relative solitude.

I discovered the first stage of the run recommended here when I mistakenly took a turn into a dead end at San Pedro Creek. This fast-flowing freshwater creek, bordered by graceful willows, is one of the last spawning areas in the county for migrating steelhead. I liked the place so much that I included it in the run.

The second stage goes along Brooks Falls Overlook Trail, which soon becomes a narrow, heavily shaded path winding through an attractive eucalyptus grove. A sign marks the direction of Brooks Falls, which drops 175 feet in three tiers during the rainy winter months.

This trail soon ends in the parking lot (total distance one and one-quarter miles), but from the footbridge on the far side of the lot a paved trail takes off and winds through the neat, structured lawns of the Walnut Grove Picnic Area to Weiler Ranch Road Trail. Weiler Ranch Road Trail travels through an open canyon with grassy meadows leading to the edge of the forest that covers the steeply rising hillside in the distance. (I was lucky enough to observe a bobcat hunting down its dinner in this meadow.)

The park is still being expanded, but already there are good restroom facilities, picnic areas and a visitor center. From a runner's standpoint, the trails are not long enough for serious training runs. In order to extend the run I once tried the Hazelnut Trail, and although it looks good on the map, the uneven, hilly path is a disaster for running. If you want a longer run you'd be better off making two loops over the trail just described.

San Pedro Valley Park is near the coast and Hwy 1, and a drive south to one of the restaurants or beaches at Montara, Moss Beach, or Half Moon Bay is a good way to spend the rest of your day. Princetown, just north of Half Moon Bay, is a good place for just "poking around." In addition to antique stores and restaurants, the side streets of the town provide a wealth of unusual sights, particularly backyards decorated with boats of various shapes and sizes, some under construction, others going to seed.

Directions to the Trail:

From Hwy 1 in Pacifica, go south-east on Linda Mar Blvd. Follow it all the way to the park. Drive past the visitor center and park.

Directions for the Run:

From the parking lot, head south on Old Trout Farm Trail, and at the fork (1), go left to San Pedro Creek, a dead-end trail (2). Return to the fork and go left on Brooks Falls Overlook Trail, following it back to the parking area, past the visitor center, to the footbridge (3). Cross the footbridge and continue on the paved path to Weiler Ranch Road Trail (4). Turn right and follow the dirt trail until it ends (5), then return to the parking lot.

Other Information:

Toilets and water fountains at start/finish. Visitor center. Possible parking fee.

Telephone numbers: San Pedro Valley Park, **(415)355-8289**; San Mateo County Parks and Recreation Dept., **(415)363-4020**.

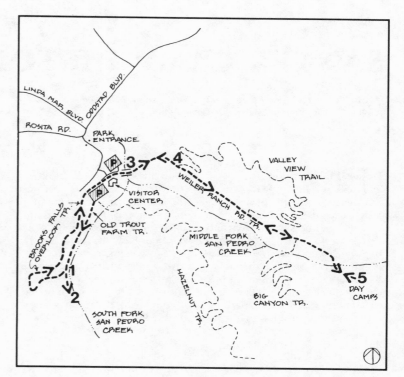

SAWYER CAMP HISTORIC TRAIL

Trail: *12 miles. Out-and-back; gently rolling; paved; 50% shade; marked every half mile. View of lakes and watershed land.*

General Description:

The Sawyer Camp Historic Trail is a 6-mile linear paved road, long closed to automobiles, which runs beside the San Andreas and Lower Crystal Springs Lakes. One of San Mateo County's designated jogging trails, this run through San Francisco watershed lands is clearly marked every half mile, well-maintained, and shaded for much of its length. It also offers some wonderful views of the lakes and the heavily wooded ridges to the west as you follow the curving hillsides above the water. The route is also relatively flat, except for the steep hill between the dam and Hillcrest Blvd.

Heading south from Hillcrest Blvd., near the large rock marking the first campsite of the Portolá expedition after they sighted San Francisco Bay, you climb one-tenth of a mile beside the freeway. Then you veer westward and down away from the noise of speeding cars until you reach the dam holding back the waters of San Andreas Lake. Crossing over the dam, you'll view the striking contrast between the glimmering expanse of San Andreas Lake to your right and the thickly forested valley below to your left.

After leaving the dam and passing through some well-shaded picnic areas, you will come to the Jepson Bay Laurel Area. If you have the time and inclination, pause awhile and read the interpretive signs posted to the right of the trail. They tell about the San Andreas Fault Zone (upon which you now stand) and the serpentine rock, indigenous to fault regions and the reason for the unusual wildflowers found here. Also discussed are bears, Indians, explorers, and the party-goers who used to assemble under the giant laurel (now the largest in California) on a regular basis almost a century ago.

After three more miles (keep your eyes open for deer—I saw five when I last ran this trail), the various trees that border the fenced trail begin to thin and Lower Crystal Springs Lake becomes clearly visible. In the summer the water's edge is surrounded by layered rings etched into the bank as the level drops, recording usage much like the rings of a tree record age. The rest of your journey to the 6-mile point at Skyline Blvd. allows a continuous view of the lake, whose waters are frequently ruffled by breezes. Sharp eyes can discern water fowl nonchalantly riding the ripples on the surface.

There isn't much here in the way of post-run activity, unless you feel like a picnic and a little leisurely lake-watching. If so, I suggest using the southern entrance to the trail at Skyline and Crystal Springs Road. From there you need walk only a short way to a bench or two which offer a gorgeous view of the lake.

Directions to the Trail:

If beginning at the north end of the trail:

Going north on Hwy 280 near Burlingame, take the Millbrae Ave. exit. Go north on Skyline Blvd. to Hillcrest Blvd., then go left under the freeway and park.

Going south on 280, take Larkspur Dr. exit. Go south on Skyline to Hillcrest, turn right, go under the freeway, and park.

If beginning at the south end of the trail:

Going north on 280, take the Hayne Road exit. Go south on Skyline to Crystal Springs Road and park.

Going north on 280, take Hwy 92 west toward Half Moon Bay Road. Turn right onto Skyline, continue to Crystal Springs Road, and park.

Directions for the Run:

From the parking area on Hillcrest Blvd. (1), go south to the dam. Cross the dam, turn left (2), follow the trail to its end at Skyline Blvd. (3), and return.

Other Information:

Portable restrooms along the route. Water and soft drinks at gas station at Hillcrest and Skyline. Picnic areas.

Begin at either the north or south trailheads or make a point-to-point with a car left at each. Another two miles can be added on a point-to-point by running the San Andreas Trail, which begins at Hillcrest Blvd. at the northernmost tip of Sawyer Camp Historic Trail (see pages 112-113).

Telephone number: San Mateo County Parks and Recreation Dept., **(415)363-4020.**

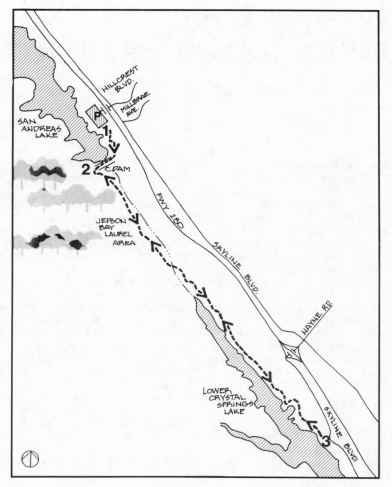

WINDY HILL
OPEN SPACE PRESERVE

Trail: *8.4 miles. Loop; hilly; dirt; shaded. Views of the South Bay. Wooded canyon; creek.*

General Description:

If you are looking for a moderately tough run in attractive surroundings, then look no further than the 702-acre Windy Hill Open Space Preserve. This is my favorite midpeninsula trail—eight miles of shaded dirt paths through cool fir- and oak-covered canyons. It offers sweet smells, impressive views, a rushing stream, and serenity, the latter being best obtained on weekdays because of the trail's growing popularity with hikers.

A one-half mile path overlooking the bay follows the curving hillside until the grass and chaparral give way to forest, and Windy Hill Loop Trail begins. From here the loop winds downhill under a tall canopy of Douglas fir and oak. From the slopes rising above, an occasional trickle of spring water crosses the trail and continues down the steep canyon to the streams below. An attraction in summer, these trickles can become a muddy nuisance in winter months.

In constant shade, the trail switchbacks move deeper and deeper into the canyon, the trees parting occasionally to allow a brief glimpse of the baylands or a neighboring hillside. For the most part, though, the surroundings are hidden from view, leaving the runner, the trail, and perhaps a deer or two in pleasant solitude. I have surprised several deer, and they provide the best excuse I can think of for taking a breather.

At the base of the canyon, which is roughly the halfway mark, you will be running beside the fast-flowing waters of Corte Madera Creek. Crossing the creek on a moss-covered stone bridge, you begin the uphill portion of the Loop Trail as it climbs above Hamms Gulch. The trail rises out of the canyon for almost two and one-half miles, with graded switchbacks making the chore somewhat easier, though by no means a piece of cake. After an unusually steep but short stretch, you will come upon a spur trail to the right. It's worth the time to follow it a few yards and peer between the trees at Palo Alto and the Dumbarton Bridge way off to the east.

The switchbacks become shorter as you near the top of the ridge, and both the climb and the Loop Trail are completed just beyond several giant Douglas fir.

For a warm-down, try taking a stroll from the north end of the picnic area to the hills that give the preserve its name. From either knoll, the absence of trees or bushes permits a wonderful view of the entire bay area, the Santa Cruz Mountains to the south, and the ocean off to the west beyond layers of rolling hills. All this is assuming that the fog, which often shrouds Windy Hill, is spending the day elsewhere. It's a good idea to bring some binoculars with you, and, if you're planning to stay for a picnic or a hike, some warm clothing is advisable—it's called Windy Hill for a reason.

Directions to the Trail:

Windy Hill Open Space Preserve is located on Skyline Blvd. (Hwy 35) about four miles north of Page Mill Road.

Directions for the Run:

From the parking lot, take the path south to Windy Hill Loop Trail (**1**) and go right. Follow the trail to the fork (**2**) and go left (the trail is marked "Windy Hill Loop Trail via Razorback Ridge Trail"). At the cinder road go left and cross the creek (**3**). Turn left again from Alpine Road to the stone bridge (**4**), cross it, and immediately turn right up the path marked Windy Hill Loop Trail. Continue uphill to complete the loop (**1**), turn right and return to the parking lot.

Other Information:

No restrooms or water. Picnic tables; kite and model plane flying.

Telephone number: Midpeninsula Regional Open Space District, **(415)965-4717.**

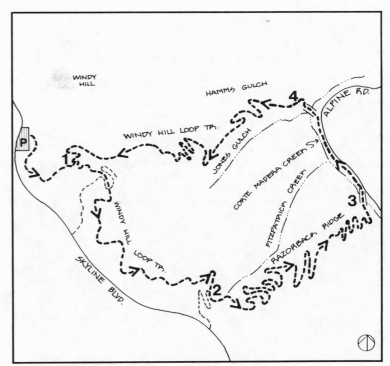

WUNDERLICH PARK

Trail: *4.6 miles. Loop; hilly; dirt; 70% shade. Hill and canyon views.*

General Description:

Located amidst the lovely homes of Woodside, Wunderlich Park's 942 wooded acres provide the runner with a series of trails varying in degree of difficulty, but all equally beautiful.

Donated to San Mateo County by contractor Martin Wunderlich, the park and the lands surrounding it have a colorful history. Alambique Creek, which flows through the park, was the power source for the first sawmill in the area and is said to have been the site of a distillery during the early logging days. Simon Jones became the owner in 1872 and cleared much of the land to build a ranch, though today only a few signs of his orchards and olive groves remain amongst the second-growth forests. In 1902, when James A. Folger II acquired the property, its character was once again altered and it became a private recreation area for his family, with riding and carriage trails following the old logger skid roads.

These days the park can be visited by all, and the county has expanded the trail system to include several routes built with runners in mind. The ten percent grading techniques, a trademark of San Mateo County, are in evidence here, allowing you to run in relative comfort through second-growth redwoods, Douglas fir, and open meadow on a very well-marked trail.

The trail goes almost a mile up a switchback path under tall redwood and eucalyptus trees—your run will be shaded by their branches and cushioned by their fallen leaves and needles. In just over two miles the route levels off and crosses a meadow, appropriately named The Meadows. At this point you have a chance to view the surrounding hillsides before beginning a refreshing downward journey, shaded once again, to the parking lot. The last leg of this run (Alambique) is a narrow equestrian trail, so watch your footing (for several reasons) and be on the lookout for approaching riders.

Near the parking lot are boarding stables and a horse ring. If you are fortunate, you may be able to watch the horses being put through their paces after you've been put through yours.

If you still feel energetic, you might try taking the trail up toward Skyline Blvd., passing through wooded canyons to the upper meadow.

Facilities are limited for other post-run activities, but you might visit nearby Woodside for a snack or go for a drive on the quiet country roads. Alternatively, you could head north to Huddart Park, another running area described in this book (see pages 106-107), where you will find more of the conventional park amenities, such as picnic areas with barbecues, and toilet facilities.

Directions to the Trail:

From Hwy 280 in Woodside, take Woodside Road west past its junction with Tripp Road, and continue on Woodside Road to the park entrance.

Directions for the Run:

From the parking lot, take Bear Gulch Trail up the switchbacks past Madrone and Redwood trails, toward The Meadows. Turn left onto Meadow Trail (1) and follow it to Alambique Trail (2). Go left to the junction with Loop Trail (3). Stay right on Alambique and follow it back to the parking lot.

Other Information:

Portable toilet and water at start/finish. Horse training area; equestrian use.

Telephone numbers: Park office, **(415)851-7570**; San Mateo County Parks and Recreation Dept., **(415)363-4020**.

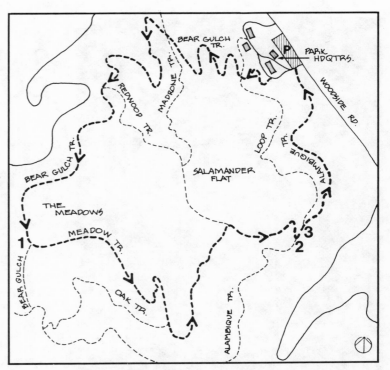

Presidio

SAN FRANCISCO COUNTY

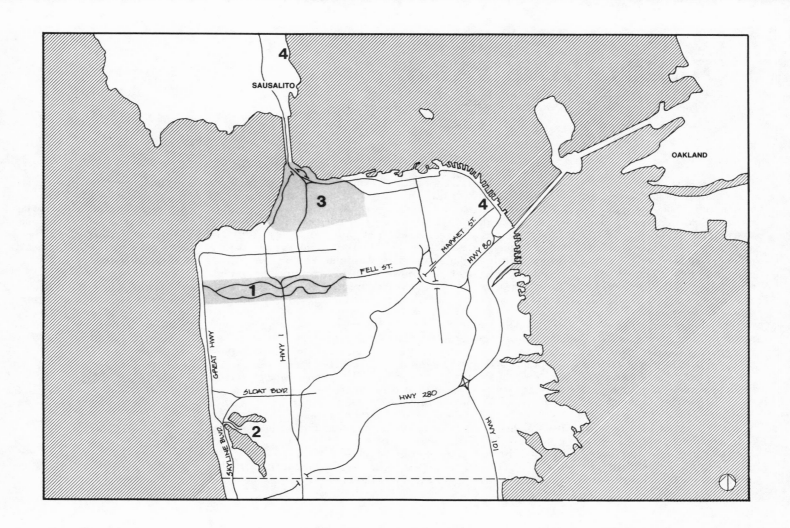

SAUSALITO

OAKLAND

4

3

4

1

2

FELL ST.

MARKET ST.

HWY 80

GREAT HWY

HWY 1

SKYLINE BLVD.

SLOAT BLVD.

HWY 280

HWY 101

GOLDEN GATE PARK

Trail: *6.3 miles. Loop; gently rolling; paved; mostly shaded.*

General Description:

Running in Golden Gate Park is as natural as singing in the shower. Colorful flower gardens, spacious meadows, and peaceful lakes are all interconnected by miles of well-surfaced trails, bike paths, and roads. Knowing these tree- and grass-covered slopes were once nothing but windswept sand dunes only makes the spectacular scenery that much more amazing. Oddly, the park did not receive unanimous support when first proposed in 1870, but today it is accepted as San Francisco's finest recreation facility. It is much more than a skillfully detailed, meticulously maintained garden-within-a-city; a variety of attractions, including a science museum (with planetarium and aquarium), art museum, polo field, ball parks and a trotting track can be found here. Naturally, such a wide variety of attractions will draw an equally wide variety of visitors. On any given day you can run amidst assorted family picnickers, roller skaters, wide-eyed tourists, impeccably dressed business people, hobos, and the last remnants of nearby Haight Ashbury's hippie era. Expect the unexpected in Golden Gate Park. It's the recreational mirror of San Francisco's amazingly complex character.

Spreckels Lake, popular with model yacht and power boat enthusiasts, will be on your right at about two miles into the run. It is followed by one of the most unusual sights found in this or any other park; the Buffalo Paddock—thirty-five acres reserved for a small herd of honest-to-goodness buffalo. Of course they don't actually "do" anything except eat, but it's thrilling just to see them there.

Just before reaching the Great Highway, another surprise awaits first-time visitors to the park: a windmill. This one, the North Mill, is surrounded by flower gardens.

Running along the Great Highway, breezes sweep off the Pacific, bringing with them echoes of the waves crashing only a few hundred feet away. Coming off the Great Highway, another windmill, Murphy's Mill, greets your return.

On the return route you will come to Mallard Lake, home to migratory ducks and a permanent nesting place for other feathered species.

After your run, the rest of the day could be well spent enjoying the many pleasures of the park. My personal favorite is the Japanese Tea Garden. What better way to relax after a run than by quietly sipping tea in an open pavilion, surrounded by the oldest Japanese-style garden in the United States. Across the way in the complex housing the science museum is a large, only slightly overpriced cafeteria, and a gift shop at which can be found information on still other park attractions.

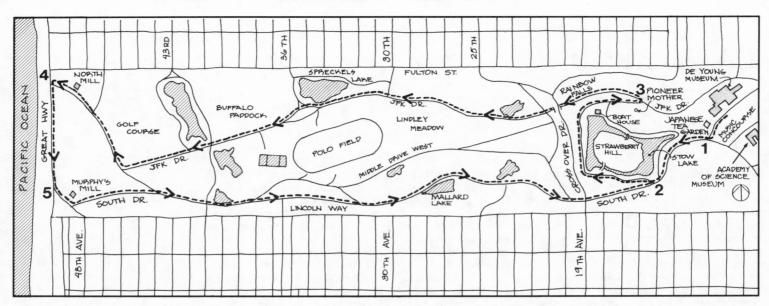

Directions to the Trail:

From Hwy 101 in San Francisco, take Fell St. exit and go west to the park entrance on John F. Kennedy Dr. Follow JFK to the Academy of Science Museum parking lot.

When JFK is closed (Sundays) turn left at the end of Fell onto Stanyan, then right onto Lincoln. At 19th Ave., enter the park and take a right on South Dr. to the parking area at the Academy of Science Museum.

Alternative: When the park is busy and parking is difficult, take Lincoln to the Great Hwy, park near the ocean and begin the run at Murphy's Windmill near Lincoln and the Great Hwy.

Directions for the Run:

Follow the one-way road from the Music Concourse past the Japanese Tea Garden to South Dr. and turn right onto the bike path (1). Go right again and take the short upward grade to Stow Lake (2). Go clockwise around the lake to the boathouse, then branch away from the lake downhill to JFK Dr. (3). The Pioneer Mother statue on your right is the 1-mile point. Turn hard left onto JFK and cross to the foot path. Go past Rainbow Falls and under Cross Over Dr. Stay on JFK all the way through the park. The road leading off to 30th Ave., opposite Lindley Meadow, is the 2-mile mark. When you reach the Great Hwy (4), you will have run 3.5 miles. Turn left onto the Great Hwy, watching out for traffic—there is no sidewalk. Go left again on South Dr. (5), following it back through the park. A horse crossing painted on the road marks 5 miles. Cross at the light at the junction with 19th Ave., staying on South Dr. The road leading off to Stow Lake marks 6 miles. From here retrace your original steps back to the Music Concourse.

Other Information:

Water and restrooms at start/finish and on route. Horse, roller skate, and boat rentals; buggy rides; museums; beaches.

Telephone number: Park Information (McLaren Lodge), (415)558-3706.

LAKE MERCED

Trail: *4.7 miles. Loop; gently rolling; paved; exposed.*

General Description:

Until the end of the 19th century, Lake Merced was not a lake at all, but a stream-fed lagoon. An accumulation of sand dunes cut off access to the ocean and created what is now a freshwater lake used as an emergency reservoir by the San Francisco Water Department. Of great interest to runners is the 4.4-mile perimeter path which has now become one of the city's favorite running spots. The atmosphere here is always jovial, with a constant stream of runners skirting the lake, while numerous other activities such as boating, windsurfing, golfing, picnicking, and kite flying are pursued within the park itself.

A run can be started at any of the many parking areas around the lake. I prefer to begin at the boathouse on Harding Road because I like to spend time there after my run. A snack bar, cocktail lounge, fishing piers, and boat rentals are all nearby.

Most of the route is bordered by automobile traffic and the noise can sometimes be a nuisance, but it is generally blotted out as your feet adopt a familiar cadence and your eyes scan the shimmering surface of the lake. In addition to the beauty of the lake itself, Mt. Sutro and Mt. San Bruno can be seen in the distance above the city rooftops.

Surrounding the lake are numerous other attractions. The Harding Park Municipal Golf Course is a public course, so if you have the energy left, it is possible to enjoy a post-run round of golf. The Pacific Rod and Gun Club on the opposite side of the lake is also open to the public. It boasts an excellent safety record, a fact which is prominently displayed at the entrance. At the north end of the lake is the San Francisco Zoo, with entrances on Sloat Blvd. and Zoo Road. Or, if you wish to do nothing but lie in the sun and watch others throw frisbees, there are ocean beaches nearby.

The peaceful setting, well-surfaced paths, cool ocean breezes, absence of serious hills, and comfortable distance, all combine to ensure that Lake Merced will continue to attract runners from all over the Bay Area. Adding to its popularity are the numerous runs and races held here, usually organized by some of San Francisco's best known running clubs.

Directions to the Trail:

From Hwy 1 in San Francisco, go west on Sloat Blvd. to Skyline Blvd. Turn left and go to Harding Road. Turn left again and park near the boathouse.

Alternative: from the Great Highway, go north on Skyline to Harding and turn right to the boathouse.

Directions for the Run:

From the boathouse on Harding Road, head along Harding toward Skyline Blvd. (1) and turn right on the bike path. At Lake Merced Blvd. (2) turn right again and head south. Skirt the large parking area at Sunset Blvd. and Lake Merced Blvd. (3) in a counter-clockwise direction back to Lake Merced Blvd. (There is another bike path that follows Sunset Blvd. two and one-quarter miles to Golden Gate Park—an easy way to add mileage to your run.) Continue south on sidewalk alongside Lake Merced Blvd., with the buildings of San Fran-

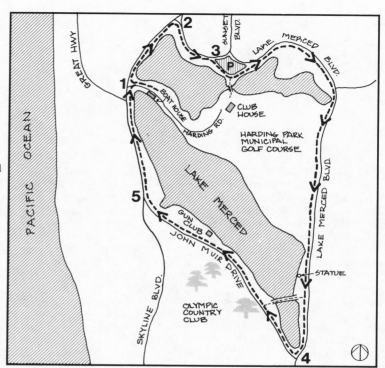

cisco State University to your left and the immaculate greens of Harding Park Municipal Golf Course to your right. The 2-mile point is closely followed by a downhill past the Lake Merced fishing pier to a curious statue by Beniamino Bufano titled "Penguin's Prayer." From here you'll see a bridge traversing the southernmost tip of the lake which you can cross if you wish to shorten your run.

Proceed to the junction with John Muir Dr. (4) and turn right. The woods leading to the Olympic Country Club will be to your left, followed by the Pacific Rod and Gun Club on your right. A gradual climb takes you to 4 miles, followed by the intersection of John Muir Dr. and Skyline Blvd. (5). Turn right and enjoy another downhill back to Harding Road, with the end point of the run, the boathouse, clearly visible across the lake. At Harding Road, turn right and retrace your steps to the boathouse.

Other Information:

Water and restrooms are at the beginning of the course. Lake; golf course; zoo; picnic area; boat rentals; beach.

Telephone number: San Francisco Recreational Parks, (415)558-4773.

PRESIDIO

Trail: *4 miles. Loop; hilly; paved; mostly exposed.*

General Description:

San Francisco's Presidio military installation was built upon 1400 acres of desolate sand dunes and hillsides. Today, thanks to a good deal of landscaping during its 200-year history, the scenery has changed. Tree-lined roads, white buildings with tiled roofs, and large, attractive gardens combine with peek-a-boo views of the city, Golden Gate Bridge, and surrounding Bay Area landmarks to make this not only a military person's dream, but also a haven for runners. With the exception of a tank used for display purposes and a few old cannons sprinkled about, the Presidio feels more like a lazy Mexican village than a military base. In fact, there's hardly a soldier in sight.

This run shows off much of the Presidio and, despite a couple of hills, is not unduly stressful. Although the roads you will be on are paved and open to traffic, they are lightly travelled, and for the most part bicycle paths will separate you from the cars.

The public is permitted, indeed welcomed, into the Presidio, and you are free to walk, bike or run through almost all the grounds. Elegant officers' quarters line the route approaching the main parade grounds, and San Francisco's earliest structure, built in 1776, is now incorporated into the Officers' Club. Pershing Square, named for World War I commander John "Black Jack" Pershing, marks the start of the annual "Presidio 10," a well-organized 10-miler which crosses the Golden Gate Bridge and returns. If you wish, you can skirt the west side of the parade grounds on Montgomery St. and inspect the brick buildings on your way. Many of the barracks date back to the turn of the century.

The Golden Gate Bridge Vista Area and Fort Point National Historic Site are both worth visiting. The vista point has a weekend gift shop where you can purchase a bottle of San Francisco "fog" or a can of Golden Gate Bridge "paint." Fort Point's visitor center is somewhat more serious, selling history books and miniature cannons. The brick fort itself is a curious building, constructed in the mid-1800s to defend San Francisco's harbor entrance. Although it quickly became obsolete, it provides an intriguing look into the Bay Area's past, and is well worth the short, steep walk from the parking lot.

Directions to the Trail:

From Hwy 101 near the Golden Gate Bridge toll booths, take the Vista Area exit onto Lincoln Blvd. and head east a short way to the Fort Point parking lot. (Parking here is free; there's a charge at the nearby Golden Gate Bridge Vista parking area.)

Directions for the Run:

From the Fort Point parking lot (**1**), go uphill on Lincoln Blvd. past the Golden Gate Bridge Vista Area (be wary of cars and tour busses in this area). Staying on Lincoln, pass under the freeway and continue up the grade. Then go downhill to Kobbe Ave. (**2**) and turn left, go past the War Memorial and turn right on Washington Blvd. (**3**). The 1-mile mark is an ocean view turnoff beyond Harrison Blvd. At Compton Road (**4**) turn left, pass through a quiet residential area and back to Washington (**5**), and turn left again. Passing the Presidio Golf Course on your right, the path climbs gradually and then turns downhill past Deems Road, the 2-mile point. Continue to Arguello Blvd. (**6**) and turn left, downhill past the officers' quarters to Moraga Ave. (**7**. Cross Pershing Square and continue through the main parade ground and parking areas to Lincoln

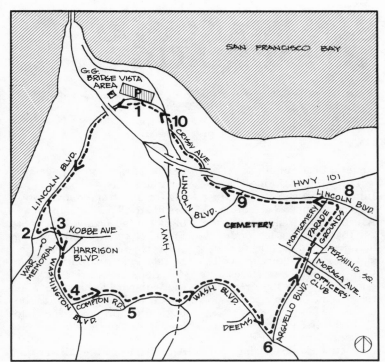

(**8**). Turn left to the sidewalk, which marks 3 miles. Lincoln climbs toward San Francisco's National Military Cemetery, then levels off and brings you back to the freeway and a junction with Crissy Field Ave. (**9**). (To avoid any further climbing it is possible to follow Lincoln all the way to the parking lot, but this is hazardous because the sidewalk peters out, forcing you to run on the busy road.) Instead, take Crissy Field Ave. steeply down under the freeway, the 3.5-mile point, past the parachute packing shop on your right, for the short trip back. The second half of Crissy Field Ave. also lacks a sidewalk, but it is possible to run beside it on a dirt path, keeping your eyes out for guide wires from nearby posts. To extend the run you can pass the parking lot and continue to the Golden Gate Bridge and across it to Marin. (See San Francisco to Sausalito run, pages 132-133.)

Other Information:

Water and restrooms at the Golden Gate Bridge Vista Area.

Telephone numbers: Presidio Army Museum, (**415**)**561-4115**; Fort Point Historic Monument, (**415**)**556-1693**.

SAN FRANCISCO TO SAUSALITO

Trail: *10.3 miles. One way (ferry return); some hills; mostly paved; 40% shade. Views of San Francisco street life, the bay, the ocean, and Sausalito street life.*

General Description:

This is one of the most beautiful runs imaginable and a fitting way to conclude a book of Bay Area running trails. It is also the run that is responsible for the "½" designation in the title, since it alone does not return us to the start—by foot anyway. Instead, we cruise back on the Bay Area's most relaxing mode of public transportation, the ferry.

On the first leg of the journey, Treasure Island is fleetingly seen between dockside buildings to the right. High to the left are Telegraph Hill and Coit Tower, and just beyond the 1-mile mark you arrive at Pier 39 and Fisherman's Wharf, arguably San Francisco's most popular tourist attraction. There is always a feeling of excitement here and some of it is sure to rub off on a runner. Street performers, horse carriages, portrait artists, and hawkers selling fresh crab and sourdough bread are all packed into a few blocks, encapsulating some of San Francisco's charm and character.

Keep running past the Hyde St. cable car turnaround, Ghirardelli Square, Aquatic Park, and the Municipal Fishing Pier. Soon the turmoil is behind you as you begin the short, steep climb into Fort Mason, the headquarters for the Golden Gate Recreational Area. Below are the old dock from which prisoners were dispatched to Alcatraz and the S.S. Jeremiah O'Brien, the only one of 2,751 Liberty ships built in World War II which is kept in its original condition. The trees surrounding you here, including Monterey cypress and eucalyptus, are not native, but were introduced by the many who have called Fort Mason their home since a cannon was first placed here by the Spanish in 1779.

Coming downhill on a dirt path and following Marina Blvd. west past the sailboats, you will find yourself in the company of scores of runners making their way around the perimeter of the Marina Green, one of the city's most popular recreation spots. In addition to joggers, the Marina Green attracts some very serious kite fliers, who perform aerobatic wonders with soaring dragons.

The Golden Gate Promenade takes you toward the mouth of the bay and the magnificent Golden Gate Bridge. Standing on the most famous bridge in the world, the vibrations from the traffic may be unsettling at first, but will soon be forgotten as you observe the windswept Marin Headlands and sailboats by the hundreds flitting between Angel Island and Alcatraz.

Coming off the bridge, you must take a heavily-trafficked road with no sidewalk for a fifth of a mile into Sausalito; this is the only unpleasant leg of the entire run. But once you are on Bridgeway, Sausalito's most renowned street, the shops, boutiques, restaurants, bars, and art galleries combine with a myriad of other establishments to create the carnival atmosphere which always permeates this town.

It can get cold quickly anywhere on the run, so I would recommend packing warm clothes. Even if you don't need them during the run, the odds are high that you'll need them out on the bay. A leisurely cruise on the ferry to the "City by the Bay" is a fitting finale for this great run.

Telephone numbers: Golden Gate Ferry (in San Francisco), **(415)332-6600; (415)543-2100** (in Marin).

Directions to the Trail:

From Hwy 80 (the Bay Bridge) going into San Francisco, take Main St. exit, turn right and continue to Steuart. Park as close as possible to the Ferry Bldg./World Trade Center at the end of Market St. Alternative: Take BART to Embarcadero Station and walk east three blocks to the Ferry Bldg.

Directions for the Run:

From the Ferry Bldg. head west on The Embarcadero past Fisherman's Wharf to Hyde (1). Go straight and follow the path around Aquatic Park to the barriers blocking the pier (2). Turn left and go up and over the hill, keeping on the dirt path, to the corner of Laguna and Marina (3). Continue beside Marina Blvd. to Marina Green (4) and use the jogging track and bike path going past the Yacht Club to reach the far end of the West Harbor (opposite Baker St.). Turn right through the small park and parking lot to the sea wall (5), and turn left onto the Golden Gate Promenade. After passing the Coast Guard Station, turn right, then left around the cyclone fence. Continue beside the water and make a hard left just past the fishing pier up Long Ave. (6). At Lincoln Blvd. (7) turn right, and at the Fort Point parking area, take the service road and go left through the

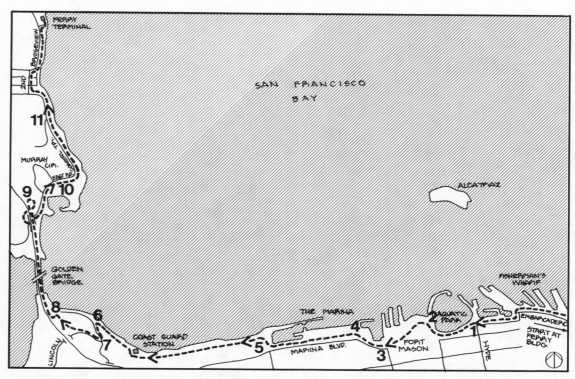

gate in the fence (8) up through the flower gardens to the Golden Gate Visitor Center. From the visitor center take the bike path across the east side of Golden Gate Bridge to Vista Point (9). Double back a few yards and take the path between the steel support girders to the west side of Hwy 101.

Make your way to the roadway and take it steeply downward, going under the highway a second time. Skirt the west side of Horseshoe Bay to Murray Circle, and turn right beside the parade grounds of East Fort Baker (10). Take East Road uphill, and continue to the stop sign at

Alexander. Veer right on Alexander (11), go downhill to Second St., and turn right. Continue for three blocks to Richardson, and turn right to Bridgeway Blvd. Turn left on Bridgeway and follow it to El Portal. Turn right and run through the parking lot to the Ferry Terminal.